S0-AUZ-520

The Wooden–Sharman Method

The Wooden – Sharman Method

A guide to winning basketball

John Wooden
Bill Sharman

with Bob Seizer

Macmillan Publishing Co., Inc.
new york

Collier Macmillan Publishers
london

Copyright © 1975 by Project Basketball, Inc.

All rights reserved. No part of this book may be reproduced or transmitted in any form or by any means, electronic or mechanical, including photocopying, recording or by any information storage and retrieval system, without permission in writing from the Publisher.

Macmillan Publishing Co., Inc.
866 Third Avenue, New York, N. Y. 10022
Collier-Macmillan Canada Ltd.

Library of Congress Cataloging in Publication Data

Wooden, John R
    The Wooden-Sharman method.

    1. Basketball.   I. Sharman, Bill, joint author.
    II. Seizer, Bob, joint author.   III. Title.
    GV885.W65   796.32'32   74-32144
ISBN 0-02-631300-6

First Printing 1975

Printed in the United States of America

Acknowledgments

We would like to extend our appreciation to the following people who have helped us in the preparation of this book:

Ira Englander and Dr. Richard Kingston of Comprenetics, Inc., Phil Jaffe and Dr. Carroll Edwards of Project Basketball, Inc.

Photographs: Wen Roberts, Photography, Inc., Inglewood, California, and Stan Troutman, Director of Photographic Services, UCLA.

Illustrations: Ray Manabe and Ed Vebell.

Graphics consultant: Jack Kinney.

Manuscript preparation: Marie Talbot, Tom Kennington and Carol Gilbert.

Consultant: Richard H. Dodge.

Contents

Preface

My relationship with John Wooden and Bill Sharman goes back twenty-five years. I came to UCLA in 1950 as a timid freshman whose one desire was to become a sports writer. John Wooden had arrived two years earlier and was already a legend. As sports editor of the *Daily Bruin* for three years, I came to know John personally, and this is one of the most cherished associations of my life.

During my undergraduate years, our cross-town rivals, the University of Southern California, had a star forward named Bill Sharman. Of course, I had no love for USC, but I did come to respect Bill as a player and a gentleman. Years later as a newspaperman for *The Los Angeles Times*, I covered Bill's celebrated career with the Boston Celtics and watched him emerge as one of the most successful coaches in professional basketball. It has been my pleasure to become his close friend off the court.

When John Wooden and Bill Sharman decided to write a basketball book and asked me to assist them in an editorial capacity, I was delighted. To me, both men epitomize dedication and sincerity and basketball know-how. The pages that follow are pure Wooden and Sharman, and I know you will share with me a sincere admiration for two giants of the game.

Bob Seizer

The Wooden–Sharman Method

Why Play Basketball?

Wooden: I met Bill Sharman almost immediately after arriving at UCLA in 1948. Bill was playing at the University of Southern California, our cross-town rival. He was the outstanding player on the basketball team and was also a fine baseball player.

Bill was a great competitor, a fighter without being a rough player. He had the spirited, competitive nature I admired, and I think his last college game is a perfect illustration of this. Bill was contending for the conference scoring championship, and in the first half, one of our players, George Stanich, had done a tremendous defensive job on him. Bill was limited to three points—all free throws.

At the start of the second half, it was announced over the public address system that George Yardley, playing for Stanford, had just broken the conference scoring record. To surpass him, Bill needed something like 18 points . . . and he had just gone through a half in which he'd been held to three points.

From that point, Bill's great competitive characteristics came through. He scored 21 points in the second half, despite the tough defensive efforts by Stanich and others. Bill Sharman wound up breaking the conference scoring record, originally held by Hank Luisetti and just broken an hour earlier by George Yardley.

In that game it was apparent to everyone what kind of competitor Sharman was. You could see the adrenalin flow, especially when they announced that the record had already been broken. It was like a slap in the face, an incentive that served to spur him on to achieve the goal he desired.

Bill went into professional basketball and became one of the most valuable players with the Boston Celtics, the team that dominated professional basketball for so many years. Bill wasn't

The only coach to win
championships in three
professional leagues, Bill
Sharman is shown here in
the first of his ten seasons
with the Boston Celtics.

blessed with the greatest speed, and he worked at developing the talents he had. He became a great shooter because he worked at perfecting his skills; he learned to move without the ball, because he knew that Bob Cousy, his teammate at Boston, would get it to him if he was open. Bill set the consecutive-free-throw record in the NBA, 56 in a row, a record that still stands. He also played professional baseball with the Brooklyn Dodgers, one of the very few athletes to combine the two sports successfully.

When Bill went into coaching, his intelligence and his competitive drive served him extremely well. He was successful at the college level, and then he moved into professional coaching. He has had championship teams in every pro league, illustrating his intelligence, his desire to succeed and his ability to work with people.

I have great admiration for Bill Sharman—from his days as an athlete and competitor and now as a coach—but even more important, I have great respect for Bill Sharman as a person. That's the main reason I am so very pleased to join with him on this project, one that I hope will be of value to others and contribute to their enjoyment of this great game of basketball.

Sharman: I often think back to when I first met John Wooden. "Encountered" is perhaps more accurate, for I was playing at Southern California, and he had just come to UCLA as the new basketball coach. I knew very well the kind of material he had at UCLA those first two seasons. I'm sure we had better personnel at USC, and I know there were other schools up and down the Pacific Coast that had better players. But John Wooden took UCLA to the championship right from the start of his career, and in reflecting on that over the years, I realized how successful he is at taking individuals and molding them into a unit. The UCLA players were not outstanding stars as individuals. But Coach Wooden made them believe in themselves, turned them into a team and they won, beating superior talent because they were able to play together.

Wooden was the first coach at that time on the Pacific Coast to emphasize the fast break consistently, and when you employ the fast-break offense, you must be in superior condition. His UCLA

*The
Wooden-Sharman
Method*

14

John Wooden, the only man to be elected to the Basketball Hall of Fame both as player and as coach, was a three-time All-American guard at Purdue University.

teams were masters of conditioning. I also learned firsthand, playing against those teams, the many advantages of quick movement, of cutting and running, of playing together as a unit.

So from the first introduction to John Wooden's theories and methods, I was impressed with the man. Since that time, and especially after I went into coaching myself, I have come to know him better and have become a friend of his.

I think there's no question on one level—John Wooden is the greatest and most successful college basketball coach who ever lived. His records are virtually unbelievable. It may be true that records are made to be broken, but I can't honestly envision anybody topping what John Wooden has accomplished at UCLA. But the thing that's even more important to me is that I admire John Wooden as a person—more than as a coach. I don't know another person, in any walk of life, who tries to do so many things right in so many areas of life. And this goes far beyond the realm of coaching. In all phases of life, on and off the basketball court, John Wooden tries his best to do the right thing. The influence he's had on the lives of the athletes and students he's coached is living testimony to the success of the man.

Another key reason I wanted to work on this project with John Wooden is that one of the most gratifying things in life is to create something new, something that will be beneficial to others. I really hope and believe that the materials produced will be useful and rewarding to others, adding to their enjoyment of the game that has meant so much to me. I feel we will be successful, primarily because of John Wooden's great knowledge, his dedication to the game and to helping others benefit from it.

Wooden & Sharman:

Why Play Basketball?

Young people growing up today have marvelous athletic facilities. At almost every level, from elementary school through high school, there are outstanding programs. Recreational activity is encouraged, there are supervised playground activities and there is usually equipment available for everyone who wants to participate.

Basketball is one sport that is truly American in development. It owes its heritage to the YMCA program and to James Naismith and other pioneers. And basketball is a sport that is still growing, perhaps more rapidly than any other.

Wooden: I was raised on a farm in Indiana and I attended a country grade school, a school that had three rooms and included students in grades 1 through 8. The school had a basketball team and a baseball team, and the principal was also the coach. He was, of course, the main teacher too. He did everything. He was a good athlete in his own right and he inspired the youngsters in this small school. I remember wanting to play both baseball and basketball, maybe even leaning a little more to baseball in those days. Because of the nature of the school, I was playing against fellows who were often four and five years older, but I think that probably helped me develop just a little bit faster.

My older brother and I shared a feeling of competing and participating, and back home on the farm we would use every chance we could get to play basketball or baseball. Of course, having a basketball was out of the question. We started with a "basketball" that was really an old cotton stocking. Mother had sewn it up for us, stuffed it with rags and made it as round as possible. We would throw that through a hoop of some sort and pretend it was a basketball. To have a real basketball was beyond our dreams, but if we could just get a rubber ball from the dime store, as close to the size of a basketball as possible, that would do. You couldn't dribble them very well but you could pretend a lot. Baseball practice was the same way; we got some rubber balls about the size of a baseball and we would throw them up against the barn, aiming for certain spots, and then we got a makeshift bat or whittled one out of a piece of hickory, and we would try to hit the rubber balls. And usually we spent more time chasing them all over the lot than we did hitting them.

But these activities, however limited in realism, had to fit into the perspective of overall life. Growing up on a farm, we never lost sight of responsibilities and assignments. Cows had to be milked and feeding had to be done, both at a certain time; the corn had to be planted at a specific time and cultivated at a certain time. And there was no putting these chores off, no waiting until later because there was a game to play. The responsibilities of the home came first. We had so much time to study and so much time to do the chores, and there was just no question about whether we would do them or not. We did them, and they were the first things we did. If we wanted to play ball, well, we just worked that in when we could.

As I look back, that was my first lesson in budgeting time and putting sports in perspective—but I certainly didn't realize it at the time.

Sharman: I started playing some type of basketball when I was about ten or eleven years old. I started on a playground near my home in Lomita, California. I remember enjoying all sports around that time, but basketball drew my attention almost from the moment I first bounced a ball. I think one of the biggest attractions it held for me was that it was a sport that I could enjoy by myself.

In those years I was somewhat on the bashful side. I was a rather introverted person, and I think this is especially true of a lot of youngsters who grow up fast, who are somewhat tall and awkward. They tend to feel self-conscious around others and have a tough time in a group situation.

Basketball is a sport that you can enjoy by yourself and work to develop your skills. You don't need teammates as you do in football or baseball, or an opponent as in tennis. So even though I was being introduced to various sports, basketball took an immediate hold on me. My father helped me build a backboard and hoop in the backyard, and I was out there practicing in the mornings and the evenings. Anytime I could get a spare minute I'd be out there shooting that ball, and if there were five minutes before dinner was ready, I'd be out there.

I had different backyard lights I would use, even though this lighting wasn't very powerful. In fact, it was more like playing in the dark. But it was still an opportunity for me to progress and develop my own skills without the help of others.

Actually, the first organized basketball that I can remember playing was in junior high school, and it wasn't the ordinary type of team play. Some of the teachers had organized a basketball league during the lunch hour. I believe we had forty-five minutes between classes for our lunch period. This became one of the favorite activities for the seventh- and eighth-graders, and even though we didn't have too much coaching, we played with tremendous intensity and enthusiasm. I remember it very strongly and this lunchtime league probably sparked the fires of competitive basketball in me.

Wooden: Growing up in Indiana, especially if basketball was a big part of your life, was different than growing up anywhere else in the country. I think the dream of almost every youngster in high school was to play on the team that won the Indiana State Championship. Maybe some young men dreamed about becoming President or owning a big corporation or making a scientific discovery. But none of those dreams could surpass the intensity or fascination felt by those who wanted to be part of a state high school championship team.

I felt those dreams too, and later I was fortunate enough to play on some teams that won the state championship. But looking back, I also feel fortunate that at the same time these dreams and realizations were taking place, I also learned about the perspective of basketball and its proper place in my life.

Probably the biggest influence in this was my father. He wanted his sons to play basketball and baseball and do the things they enjoyed. But there was never any question about the importance of athletics or how sports related to the family life and other responsibilities. My high school was eight miles away and that was quite a distance to travel in those days. And we always had chores to do in the morning and evening, and we had to learn that nobody was going to do our work for us. Basketball, baseball, whatever the activity, had to fit in after everything else was done.

I think the athletes who have played for me at UCLA know how I feel about the role of basketball and the influence it has in their lives. They enrolled at UCLA for one purpose—to get an education. That's the only reason they are there. If they aren't interested in an education, they should not be in college. I'm extremely proud of the fact that we probably have as high a percentage of our basketball players getting their degrees as can be found at any university in the country. I'm proud of it, and it's not just by chance that this has happened. I work hard to get the idea across to our players that the main reason they're at UCLA is to get an education, and I make sure they know I'll be very disappointed if they don't go on to get their degrees. I don't want them to feel that playing basketball, that winning conference titles and national championships, is everything in life. If they put that above everything else, it will get completely out of perspective and they will tighten up, and they'll want to win so badly that nothing will seem to go right for them.

Keeping basketball or any sports activity in the proper perspective is a tough job. Self-analysis is very difficult. For example, I don't encourage my players to play summer basketball at all. Some of the greatest players that I've coached never touched a basketball from the time one season ended until the next one began. And some of the greatest players I've had played every day during the summer months. What it means is that individuals have to make decisions for themselves. What is right and proper for one man isn't necessarily right for another.

I try to get my players to realize that basketball is *not* the one and only thing in life. I like what Charlie Brown, the character in "Peanuts," says: "Winning isn't everything, but losing is nothing." I think there's something to that. I want my players to play to win and I want them to work hard to develop their skills to the highest degree they can. We're not created equal, we're not all endowed with the same talents. Some are going to be better in basketball, some are going to be better in other endeavors of life. But if you can develop yourself and achieve satisfaction that you've done the best you could, then that's the most you can ask. Winning and losing will take care of themselves. Life goes far beyond the scoreboard of a basketball game.

2 Player and Coach

Wooden & Sharman:

Sometimes one of the most difficult lessons to learn is how to relate to the coach. Outwardly, this doesn't seem like a problem at all. The coach is the man in charge, the figure of authority and knowledge. Yet some young men aren't as willing to accept this as others. They question the coach's methods, his manner of offensive and defensive strategy, the way he substitutes, everything he does.

Right from the outset, the player must understand that incorrect judgment is going to hurt the coach more than anyone else. It's not the player's job that's on the line, it's the coach's job. If his evaluation and use of material isn't good, someone else will probably be the basketball coach next year.

The player's job is to be attentive, to understand thoroughly what the coach is trying to accomplish. If you don't understand a certain phase of the game or a certain strategy, then ask questions and make sure you know exactly what the coach is trying to get across. And always keep in mind that the coach is looking at it from a team standpoint. He doesn't see individuals; he sees members of a team and how they fit into the unit to give it strength.

If you're sitting on the bench and griping inwardly about not getting to play more, it's going to affect you when you do get in the game. You're not going to be able to perform up to your capabilities when called upon. What you should be doing is studying what is happening on the court. You probably know the man you'll be replacing. Study his play, study his opponent and be ready to take advantage of anything and everything you see while sitting on the bench. If you're sitting there unhappy and complaining to your teammates about not playing, you're certainly not going to be able to do the job when the coach needs you. You won't be able to help the team.

Sharman: The most important thing in learning the game of basketball is to get involved. When I was in junior high and later in high school, I would pretend that I was the coach or the key player in certain situations. While I was sitting on the bench I would visualize these situations and I would ask myself what I would do if I got the ball . . . or what play I'd run if I were the coach.

Later, when I was playing in college and then in the pro ranks, I would keep a notebook handy. I would analyze my opponents, which ones I could overplay to one side or another, which ones were slow getting back on defense, which ones I could drive on, which ones to foul because they were poor foul shooters, and so on.

One of my recent Laker players, Jimmy Price, came in as a rookie with a lot of ability, but he had a tremendous amount to learn. He spent most of his first season sitting on the bench. I suggested to him that he keep a notebook on his own performance, and also keep notes on opponents, analyzing them in every department. Jimmy did that, and in his second year he got to play a great deal and he played extremely well. He's going to be a star in the NBA for many years, and a large part of it is that he was willing to spend that extra work to get there. He had the dedication and desire; that may be a cliché, but there's no substitute for those qualities.

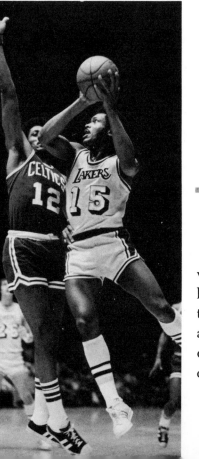

During his rookie year in the NBA, Jim Price took his coach's advice and kept a careful record of his own play as well as that of his opponents. Dedication and desire have paid off for Jim.

Wooden & Sharman:

The coach who is successful is interested in finding the right way, not interested in always having his own way. Most of the time he's going to do things his way because he has the experience and the knowledge. But there's always room for questions and appraisals. When a player has an honest question, something that he doesn't understand, he should certainly not be afraid to ask the coach about it.

A coach wants spirited basketball players, young men who are willing to sacrifice for the team. A coach doesn't want temperamental players who second-guess every move and inwardly gripe about conditions that don't suit them. But when a player has something to offer to make the team better, then the coach is certainly going to listen to it.

Wooden: I remember one particular incident when I was coaching high school basketball in South Bend, Indiana. The young man involved was Jimmy Powers, and on one play in practice he didn't do it the way I wanted. So I stopped practice and said, "Now, Jimmy, I've told you to take your man out of there when our guard drives through." Jimmy said, "Coach, I tried to. I went out, but he didn't come with me." Now that put me on the spot. I guess I could have been upset and ranted about doing it my way, but fortunately, I didn't do it—not that time anyway. I thought about it for a moment . . . and Jimmy was right. So I changed my coaching strategy, and from then on I told my forwards, instead of taking their man out, to go to the basket as hard as they could. If their man floated over to stop the play—then they would be wide open for a pass. This basic change in my coaching strategy came from a comment by a player who wasn't afraid to speak up and tell me what he thought; he helped me become a better basketball coach.

Incidentally, that young man, Jimmy Powers, later became head coach at the same high school where I coached him.

Wooden & Sharman:
One of the hardest lessons for any player to learn is to have confidence in the coach's judgment. It's the coach's job, his responsibility, to put out the best basketball team. He doesn't play the five

men he likes the best. It probably never happens that way. He has to reach beyond individual personalities and personal likes or dislikes. He tries to coordinate the best personnel for the sake of the team. It's often very difficult for the individual player to accept a certain role, to understand what the coach is trying to accomplish. When these uncertainties arise, when there's a tenseness between you and the coach, then it's best to air it, ask the coach what he expects of you and where you can improve. Don't get sullen or turn inward or do things you'll later come to regret.

Wooden: There was one time in my high school career that I quit the team and thought I had given up the game for good. When I was a freshman, my older brother was on the varsity and he was a very good player. But the coach never started him. He used him as the sixth man, putting him in at either guard or forward. And when he went in he played exceptionally well, usually a lot better than the man he replaced. But the coach never started my brother, and I just couldn't understand it.

When I came up to the varsity the next year I had a slight argument in practice one day with one of the starters on the team —the outstanding player on the team, in fact. The coach stopped us and admonished both of us. But I was very spirited and naturally I thought I was right and the other fellow was all wrong. I thought the coach should have blamed him entirely. I didn't like it and I just turned and said to him, "You're not going to treat me like you did my brother." I then walked off the floor and, being stubborn or spirited or whatever you want to call it, I just quit the team.

Well, I was eating my heart out. I wanted to play basketball more than anything else, but I was stubborn. The coach kept coming to talk to me, and I think he did it every day. After a week or so I finally relented and came back to the team. I felt then I was right. But I was wrong. I never understood until many years later, when I got into coaching myself, how valuable a sixth man can be. The team has to come first and as I look back now I can see that the way the coach handled my brother was in the best interest of the team.

And I often wonder where I would be today if my high school coach hadn't kept pursuing me, asking me to come back to the team. He didn't let stubbornness or pride interfere with his handling of an individual. I've often reflected on this incident and how it affected my life, and it's helped me many times deal with similar situations in my coaching career.

3 Attitude—Desire

When you watch basketball players on television or in person, you're bound to be impressed by their marvelous skills. They seem to be able to make every kind of shot; they have fantastic speed and endurance, wonderful agility, coordination and strength. And they make it look so easy, so natural. But then when you step on the court yourself . . . it all seems so different, so difficult. The moves and techniques you made in your dreams don't seem possible in real-life situations.

It takes time to develop skills in any field. This is especially true in athletics, where so many different talents and abilities have to be combined. It's easy to get discouraged and drop out. Progress may be slow, and you may not be improving your skills as rapidly as you'd like. You may not be playing very much, and you may be seeing your friends move along and improve at a much faster pace.

The surest way to grow strong is to meet adversity. Learn to cope with it, gain from the experience, whip the problems and don't let them control you. Everyone has problems and obstacles to overcome. It's how you face these adversities that will determine what you do in life and in sports.

Wooden: I remember a particular season when a number of things built up that were very disappointing to me. We were winning and having a fine year, but there were a lot of problems with players, personal problems that were very discouraging to me. I don't dream very much, but one night my father came to me in a dream. He was so close I felt I could reach out and touch him. I said to him, "Dad, it's so difficult, I just don't know which way to turn. I just don't know if it is worthwhile. Maybe I should get out of coaching." He looked at me and said, "Son, since when

Bill Russell and Darrall Imhoff, two players who had trouble making their high school basketball teams. Refusing to give up, Russell went on to become one of the most dominant players in the history of the game, and Imhoff to a career with several professional teams.

have you gotten around to believing that life itself is supposed to be easy?"

I woke up with a start soon after and that's all I can remember. But I got the point. That incident one night a few years ago made the realities of life very clear to me. Life is not easy . . . and it was never meant to be.

Adversity has played a large role in shaping the careers of some of basketball's greatest players. The case of Bill Russell is a perfect example. In high school, in Oakland, California, Bill went out for basketball in his sophomore year. He was cut from the team.

He tried again as a junior. He was cut again. But he didn't give up. He worked on his own, playing in pickup games on playgrounds in the summertime. Finally he was able to make a church team, getting the chance to play with other young men and develop his timing and basketball instincts.

Finally, in his senior year in high school, he made the team. The hard work, the perseverance had paid off . . . but even then he was far from being a star. He received only one scholarship offer—to the University of San Francisco, hardly a basketball power at the time. The school didn't even have a practice gym; it had to use the facilities of a nearby high school.

But Bill Russell had learned what hard work and dedication could accomplish. He led the USF team to two national collegiate championships, 60 straight victories at one stretch . . . and as everyone knows, Russell later led the Boston Celtics to 11 NBA titles in 13 years.

Russell certainly isn't the only star player who had to overcome adversity. George Mikan, who was voted the greatest basketball player in the first half of this century, was just a big, awkward youngster in high school. He didn't even appear destined to make it to a college team. But Mikan was determined; he spent hour after hour practicing by himself, sometimes shooting a thousand hook shots a day, both right- and left-handed. He improved his footwork and body coordination, and later starred in college at De Paul and then led the Minneapolis Lakers to five straight NBA titles.

Bob Pettit was cut from his high school squad, and it would have been easy for him to give up. He was a shy, awkward youth who didn't have much confidence. But he was determined. He worked hard on his own and became one of the greatest players ever to play the game.

Even when players have natural ability, it's the hard work that makes them great and sets them apart from the others. Jerry West, for example, grew up in a very small town in West Virginia. He didn't have the opportunity to work out in a gym whenever he wanted or even to work with other boys his own age. So he had a hoop in his backyard; it wasn't even a regulation basket and net, just sort of a homemade hoop. He would go out there and practice for hours by himself. A lot of times it was so dark he would get a lantern or any kind of light just so he could see the ball and the hoop. He worked to develop his skills and he would visualize himself bringing the ball down the court, maybe the last ten or twenty seconds of a ball game. He would imagine what he would have to do in that situation, what maneuver to use, what kind of shot to take.

It's easy to understand now why Jerry West became known as Mr. Clutch, the man who always seems to come through with the winning basket in the crucial situations. And Jerry has said he actually prefers to have the ball in those pressure situations, to have everything depend on his performance. He has the confidence and the ability to get the job done. That early training, the formative mental and physical training he put himself through in his schoolboy years in West Virginia may have been among the most important lessons he ever learned.

There are many other examples of players who refused to give up when the odds seemed stacked against them. Darrall Imhoff had such an undistinguished high school career that he didn't get a single college scholarship offer. But he was determined to become an outstanding basketball player, and he worked hard during the summers and went out for the University of California team on his own. He managed to make the squad. He asked coach Pete Newell for as much advice as possible and, by the time his junior year rolled around, Imhoff was a starter. That season California won the NCAA championship—and the next year they went to the finals, before losing to Ohio State. Both California teams were built around the great defensive work of Imhoff.

Later, the prevailing opinion was that Imhoff couldn't make it in professional basketball. But he wasn't about to be defeated. Those habits of work and discipline were ingrained in him. Darrall had a fine career in the NBA, playing for twelve years and appearing in the championship finals with his team on three occasions.

Many of the players mentioned fit into a certain category—tall and awkward in their teens, slow to acquire coordination and body control. There are just as many, perhaps more, in another category— the small youngsters, those who become discouraged by their lack of height, and by everyone telling them they're too short to go any further in the game of basketball.

One player who didn't listen to that was Gail Goodrich. As a junior in high school, when players start to be recruited heavily, Goodrich was 5 feet 7 inches and weighed about 135 pounds. Instead of giving up because of this, Gail decided he had to work harder and develop more skills than the players he was facing. He did grow some in his senior year and made the All-City team in Los Angeles. But still the college recruiters virtually ignored him. When Goodrich got to UCLA, he knew he had to continue to work harder and play smarter than others who were bigger and stronger. It certainly paid off. Gail became an All-American, played on our first two national championship teams, and has gone on to become an All-Pro in the NBA.

Wooden: Two of the finest players that I've ever had as far as making the most of their own abilities are men who weren't very well known by the general public. They weren't superstars like Kareem Jabbar or Bill Walton or Gail Goodrich or Sidney Wicks.

One was Conrad Burke, who was not blessed with a great deal of physical ability. He wasn't very big and he wasn't very quick. He was somewhere in the middle of the talent range. But he learned the fundamentals, he listened and he applied himself. He learned to do the things he could do, and he didn't try to do things he knew he couldn't accomplish. In that way he became a very proficient player, a steady, consistent performer who nearly always played to the highest level of his ability.

Another player was Doug McIntosh, a young man who wasn't endowed with great natural ability. But he paid the price in

Doug McIntosh is a player who made the most of his abilities because he learned the fundamentals and executed them well. He worked hard in college and played a big part in UCLA's success, even though many players had more natural talent.

working hard to get the most out of the ability he had, and he never worried that others might be more talented or score more points or get more publicity. Doug McIntosh started every game for me and was one of the most valuable men on the UCLA team that won the national championship in 1965. And I'm just as proud of players like Conrad Burke and Doug McIntosh as I am of those who went on to become all-time greats in professional basketball.

Wooden & Sharman:

The players who are blessed with natural talent become the stars in basketball, much as in any other sport. But the players who become the great ones are those young men who possess natural talent, and then work hard to develop their skills even further.

An example is Pete Maravich. His father was a basketball coach and Pete took to the game with natural instincts. He was a great shooter, capable of getting off every possible type of shot he could dream up or imagine. He was a leading scorer at every level . . . and at Louisiana State University he set scoring records that surpassed those of the great Oscar Robertson.

But Pete Maravich also worked hard at his ball-handling and dribbling techniques. His father says when Pete went to the store on an errand he would take a basketball with him, dribbling it down the sidewalk and street. When he went to the movies, Pete would take a basketball with him, and he would sit on the aisle and practice dribbling and maintaining control of the ball. Midway through the movie he would switch seats, sitting on the other aisle to practice dribbling with his other hand.

Maravich would have reached the highest basketball levels on his shooting ability—and he could have gone on practicing that phase of the game, knowing the ball would come to him. But he was determined to be a playmaker also, and his work on passing, dribbling and overall court sense has made him one of the game's most exciting performers.

The Wooden-Sharman Method

32

Pete Maravich's father, a successful college coach, claims that as a youngster his son was seldom without a basketball. He dribbled and practiced ball control while he walked to school or on an errand for his parents. He even slept with a basketball!

Sharman: Bob Cousy is probably the best dribbler and playmaker who ever played basketball. Most people probably think these skills came naturally to Cousy. Some of them did, of course, but I was fortunate to be Cousy's teammate and roommate for ten years with the Boston Celtics, and I know how hard he worked to perfect these talents. He would often go to a gym all by himself and spend two or three hours working on his dribbling. He used to put on a blindfold, training himself not to look at the ball when he was dribbling. He wanted fingertip control at all times in a game, and he wanted to be able to keep his eyes and head up, have overall vision and be able to see and hit the open man.

Cousy was the first to really use the behind-the-back dribble. Now it's quite common, but Bob was the first to make effective use of it. He told me it came about when he was playing at Holy Cross and an opponent was guarding him so closely he couldn't maneuver. So the behind-the-back move came about instinctively. Then he worked hard on it. He would go to a gym, again by himself, and race down court near the wall. He would practice the move over and over. He would pick out a spot on the wall and pretend it was a teammate. He would fix his eyes on the EXIT sign . . . and pass the other way. Bob Cousy made things look easy, and everyone marveled at what he could do with a basketball. Even other players couldn't believe some of the things he did. But I can guarantee you, from personal experience, Bob Cousy worked very, very hard at making these moves look easy and natural.

4 Player Relationships

Wooden & Sharman:

In every team sport, not just basketball, the individual must always remember that the team is the main idea. Every player wants to score baskets, and that's a natural desire. It's the object of the game. But when the individual starts to put his own statistics ahead of the team, it's going to make the team much weaker and create losing situations.

If team play can be simplified into one word, it would be "consideration." You have to be considerate of others, not just your teammates, but the team manager, the trainer, custodian and others. Practicing consideration off the court will make it a habit on the court. A player who is not considerate of others is not going to be a good team player in any sport. Now that doesn't mean that some individuals won't be more talented or score more points than others. But consideration takes many forms. It will show up in dressing rooms, where the player won't leave his clothes around for someone else to pick up. He won't leave towels thrown around, or orange peels on the floor, or toss gum wrappers around. The players who are not considerate of others are the ones who are usually not as good team players as they might be. In some instances, there will be players seeing a lot of action who are not outstanding team players. They are in the game because they have so much ability it outweighs their lack of team play. But as a player goes higher in the levels of competitive basketball he will, of necessity, acquire a sense of team play, and this will help make a good player a better one, an outstanding player a great one.

The Wooden-Sharman Method

34

Wooden: I feel that baskets should be scored as the result of passing the ball and moving without the ball, rather than the man with the ball trying to get the shot for himself, dribbling to get himself clear. I tell my players that when they have the ball, the first thing they should look for is the pass. The second thing is to take advantage of a defensive mistake that may leave them free to drive. And when the man guarding them makes a defensive mistake, and another man comes over to cover, I want my players to realize instantly and instinctively that a teammate is open for a pass.

Team unity and cohesion are the most important goals. That doesn't mean that all the players have to like each other and be buddy-buddy off the court. In fact, I think it's impossible to expect to like all players equally. You're going to be friendlier with some teammates than others, and when practice and games are over, you can each go your separate ways. But the important thing is not to let your personal likes and dislikes affect the harmony and unity of the team.

Wooden & Sharman:

While there are just five starting positions on a basketball team, there is a place for everyone on the team. It's up to the coach to determine what niche the player will fill. One player may be a starter and play virtually the entire game. Another player's role might be to play ten minutes a game. Another player might come in off the bench to fire up the team when it needs movement or is playing lethargically. Another player may hardly ever get into a ball game until it is won or lost, but what he does during practice each day and the support he gives toward the development of those who are playing more is essential. Every winning team must have this sense of unity and dedication.

Consideration of others is extremely important in making yourself a better basketball player, and in making your team better. Try to understand the other fellow's role. If you're on the starting five, put yourself in the position of the tenth man on the team, the guy who isn't playing a lot. If you're one of the reserves, try to understand the role of the starter. Don't be there just to compete with him, though. You're there to be part of the team and you want the team to become as strong as it possibly can. You're not out there to beat out Jim or Tom or Joe.

You may not agree with the way the coach is using his personnel. There's one way to change his mind: show him on the practice floor, with a little more determination and by working even harder. You're not going to win a job by griping to teammates or hanging your head or continually asking your friends why so-and-so is playing so much more than I am.

Sharman: When John Havlicek joined the Boston Celtics he discovered it wasn't going to be so easy for him to find a spot. He came from a strong team at Ohio State, but he was joining a championship professional team. Havlicek's skills were still unpolished. So John, on his own, worked on his weaknesses. He reported earlier and stayed later than other players. In the summers he often worked out for five and six hours at a time. He had the desire. He wanted to become a part of the team. Also, his relationships with older and wiser teammates were excellent. They talked and he listened. His eagerness to become a contributing Celtic and his courteous manner in listening to the team veterans gained their respect and confidence. At first he was used as a sixth man, and he was outstanding in this role. He always seemed to pick up the team and get them moving. In later years, John Havlicek became a starter, and through his hard work and determination, he became one of the all-time greats in pro basketball.

Wooden & Sharman:

When you're in a team situation, you're going to spend hours and hours together. You're going to endure strain and tension and there are going to be some people who respond to this in different ways than others.

John Havlicek made the transition from college to pro ball because he was willing to listen to and learn from his veteran Celtic teammates. His brilliant career is the result of hard work and determination.

In every sport there's a certain amount of needling and horseplay that goes on. The coach might encourage it, or even do it himself if he feels that certain players need prodding to play their best. Sometimes a coach might call the name of a substitute, just as the man in the game runs by the bench. That might have the desired effect on one type of player. On another, it might make him play scared and tense, and it would be detrimental to the team.

As far as practical jokes are concerned, they are often very funny —but hard to forget. If an individual has to be the butt of the practical joke, make sure you can take it yourself. Make yourself the butt of the joke, rather than your teammate.

Wooden: We once had a player who was deathly afraid of snakes. Everybody on the team knew about this fear. One time, on a road trip, some of the fellows caught a snake and put it in his bed just before he slipped between the sheets. This young man was a very sensitive person and very spirited. He reacted in a violent manner and went so far as to swear he'd kill the guy who did it if he ever found out. When he got himself under control, he asked his teammates not to tell him who had played the joke, because he didn't want to be responsible for the actions he might take. This incident created tension on the team for a long time after that. It might have been an insignificant gag, but not to the young man involved.

Wooden & Sharman:

Players fall into categories when it comes to needling, and so do coaches. Some players take kidding and needling easily, not letting it penetrate or harm them in any way, and others don't. Fortunately, most players sense who can take it and who can't. And so do the coaches.

Sharman: Red Auerbach, my coach with the Boston Celtics, was a great cigar smoker. It got to be a habit of his that whenever we had a game under control, he would light up on the bench. He also had a penchant for flicking cigar ashes on people's shoulders or in their hair. Tommy Heinsohn was one of Red's favorite victims. But Tommy could take it. He didn't object to being the butt of the joke, and it was one of the things that kept our team so loose. One night, Tommy figured it was time for revenge. He bought one of those exploding cigars, and he made sure it was a game that we could control. We got a pretty good lead in the fourth quarter, and Red reached in for the cigar and began puffing away contentedly . . . when all of a sudden, it went off. The players on the bench knew about it, and so did most of the men on the court, and we were paying more attention to the cigar than we were to the action in the game. It was a great laugh, one we remembered and talked about for a long time. The Boston Celtics were a loose team and a winning team, and everything fit together. Red Auerbach went on dropping ashes on Tommy Heinsohn and we continued to win. Today, Heinsohn is the coach, Auerbach is president and general manager of the club. Practical jokes, kidding, needling—they can be helpful and beneficial . . . but you must know the personalities involved and how each will react.

5 Consideration of Others

Wooden & Sharman:

Not everyone who plays basketball gains fame or notoriety. However, most athletes get attention they might not have received had they not gone into sports. You'll find that if you play on your school team, you'll become better known around campus and in your own neighborhood. People will come to watch you perform. The school newspaper may write feature articles about you. A certain aura seems to surround the athlete, more now than ever before.

It's easy for a young man to lose perspective. It's easy to attach a large degree of importance to yourself, to accomplishments you see in print or in a box score in the newspaper. Sometimes it's very easy to forget that the world will keep turning without every one of us. Whether you're a superstar or a sandlot player, you must remember that you're a person just like everyone else. Some have talents in one field, some in another. No one deserves special treatment or favors just because of his ability to stuff a basketball in a hoop or dribble behind the back.

Wooden: The time you spend playing basketball makes up a very small portion of your life. I try to get the idea across to my players that you're as good as anyone else, but you're no better than anyone else. The team managers are not servants. They are there to help, but not to pick up gum wrappers that players throw around or orange peels tossed away without thinking. I want things put in their proper place—as a matter of courtesy and thoughtfulness. It's just simple consideration for others, and these examples may seem trifling and small, but to me they loom very large in the way I look at players and how they will fit into my team.

I try to emphasize that the way we play as a team, in the intense competition of a game, is in direct proportion to the way we think of others—on and off the basketball floor. A person doesn't *suddenly* become a team person. You work at it. It becomes an instinct . . . it will happen naturally . . . and then you find you don't have to work at it. It's consideration and concern for others. That's what team play is all about. It's almost impossible to be inconsiderate off the floor . . . and then turn around and be considerate of others in a basketball game. That's why I consider what happens in the locker room or in the classroom a very meaningful barometer of what is going to happen in a game.

Sharman: It's important to be aware of not trying to take advantage of others and not trying to be boastful. A basketball player should be humble about his athletic accomplishments, rather than boastful. I think he will get a lot more respect from his friends if he takes things in stride. Sports is something to share, to be proud of, without the need to overemphasize a personal role.

I believe one of the strongest philosophies I have in life is that gaining and enjoying friends is probably the most important factor in life, outside of religion and your own immediate family. I think that if a player lets basketball go to his head, this can be a serious problem and can turn his teammates off and certainly jeopardize his relationships with friends, lasting friends who could be very close to him for years to come. Looking back, I think that my closest friends throughout the years were my high school friends, even though we split and went our separate ways. But those friendships, formed through and around athletics, are the ones that have lasted the longest.

Wooden & Sharman:
Sports has a reputation for "special privileges" for athletes, especially college athletes. It's often insinuated that athletes can "get away with things" in school, and the bigger the headlines, the more favors and special considerations the athlete reportedly gets. If an athlete is to take pride in himself, however, it's important to have

the self-respect that will not tolerate the taking of special privileges.

Professors should have consideration for student-athletes in regard to particular requirements, like road trips that take the student away from his classes. But that doesn't mean the instructor has to give away anything. It's the responsibility of the student to make sure he doesn't fall behind. Getting along with instructors and fellow students means being treated the same way everyone else is. And in the long run you'll be glad you didn't demand special favors or other considerations.

Sharman: Self-discipline is an important part of basketball, and it carries over into the classroom. One helps the other. There's a great similarity between those who get the job done on the court, and those who get their homework done in school. A student should not take advantage of being on the team. He should make arrangements ahead of time with his teacher when there are road games coming up or assignments that will be missed. I'm sure most teachers will readily understand. This is where self-discipline comes in—the athlete must work his school requirements around basketball. It should be very clear which one comes first.

Wooden & Sharman:

Sports is a very popular activity, so usually a player motivates himself to take part in athletics. It's possible, however, that some players may be pushed into sports by parental pressure.

Consideration of Others

It's important that parents lend encouragement and most of the time this will surely be the case. Every parent has a natural desire to see his child excel and become an outstanding player. But the young man or woman must have the desire to participate. The impetus can't come solely from the parent. Every coach has seen the child

41

who's been pushed hard to play. Those children, unfortunately, don't get very lasting values from their involvement in athletics.

Even when the decision to participate is left solely to the student, there is another consideration. The parents have to guard against being supercritical, making it so important in life that the young man doesn't even want to play in front of his parents, for fear of embarrassing himself. The decision to play should be his. The desire to do well should also be his.

The role of the parents should be positive and helpful, not critical and aggressive. This is where communication is so important. A close relationship with your parents will help both them and you to understand each other's feelings. Here again, this isn't just important for playing basketball. It's important to communicate as human beings.

While parents have to be careful about applying undue pressure and being too aggressive about their son's involvement in sports, the young man has to use caution and common sense too. He can't burden his family with problems arising from basketball or any other sport. It's not being considerate to complain and cry all the time about what the coach is doing or about the way the team is playing. This doesn't mean you don't talk about things at home. Communicating with your family is of tremendous value, one of the enriching joys of family life. You can ease the tensions of basketball, as well as of everyday life, by talking things over with your parents. But don't turn to them for support because you're not playing or because you want to hear how good you are and that the coach really doesn't appreciate you. That's not the role for parents. If it occurs, and unfortunately it does, it endangers a healthy family relationship in many ways.

If basketball is important to you, it will probably take a lot of your time. This can interfere with your family life. Remember, your family comes first—as well as your duties and chores at home. Self-disciplined athletes usually are considerate enough toward other people to schedule their activities around family plans. On the other hand, if parents truly understand that basketball is important to their son, they'll probably allow their plans to become adjustable. But it's a two-way street. They'll adjust if you adjust, so there again, communication is the key.

Sharman: I think unity is important for the team, and it also blends into the family situation. There has to be consideration and understanding on the part of both parent and son. I think it's important to carefully plan schedules. Parents who are interested in their son's activities can plan their schedules to attend games, help with his diet and sleep and make sure his chores are planned around his playing schedule. But I think it's important for the player not to take advantage of the situation. He shouldn't attempt to escape his family responsibilities.

Wooden & Sharman:

In a natural family relationship, a son has a great deal of respect for his father. Perhaps he started playing basketball because his father once played the game, and maybe played it very well. But the son is starting his own venture into the sport, as well as into life.

It's important that the young athlete learn the game in his own dimension and independently establish his own habits, his own self-discipline. It's okay for a player to take advice from his father, but it only makes for an awkward situation when the player fails to listen to his coach or goes against the concepts the coach is trying to get across. There might be times when a coach gives instructions that are just the opposite of the way his father has taught him. Don't say, "Dad said do it this way" or "My dad does it better than that." The coach should be open to suggestions, but it's important to remember he's the man in charge. He may have ways of doing things that seem out of balance, but he's doing it because he feels it works. He's there because of experience and expertise. The player must be careful not to antagonize him. It's perfectly all right to ask why things are being done this way or that way . . . and to make suggestions. But do it tactfully and respectfully.

Consideration of Others

While the athlete shouldn't make awkward situations for the parents and coaches, the parents have to guard even more strongly

43

about getting too involved with the coach and the athlete. Interference by the parent in the player-coach relationship seldom builds anything positive. It usually leads to unfortunate results.

Wooden: In my early years of high school coaching, I did something which I'm still very ashamed and sorry about. We had on our squad a young man who was a very hard worker. He hadn't played enough to earn a letter, but we had a school board that made the final decision. I knew they would award a letter to anyone whom I recommended and I had already decided in my own mind that this young man deserved a letter, even though by the strict interpretation of the rules he didn't qualify.

One day the young man's father came into my office and without hardly a word of greeting he said, "Wooden, is Joe going to get a letter?" I said, "Well, I'm considering it, as you know, but he doesn't have enough playing time." He pointed his finger at me and said, "Well, he had better get a letter or I'll have your job."

I told him to get out. In those days I was young and a fighter, and I decided in the heat of that incident that I would NOT recommend him. And I didn't.

I had made up my mind to give the young man a letter, but when his father confronted me so strongly, I let my emotions affect my judgment. Later I tried to change the award list but it was too late and the young man never got his letter. I've always regretted that and am ashamed of what I did. It became a lasting lesson to me as a coach.

6 **Playing with Intelligence**

Wooden & Sharman:

As a basketball player, you're involved in a physical sport. Improving your body control, coordination, reflexes and strength are so obvious that many players make the mistake of refining just these elements. But basketball is just like other aspects of life—you've got to use your head. The mental elements of the game are crucial to your performance, and even if you don't make basketball the most important part of your life, you'll find that thinking your way through basketball will help you use your mind to better advantage all through your life.

Many games are lost because players don't pay attention to the overall floor situation. Maybe it will be ignoring an open man or making a turnover like going over-and-back across the center line or forgetting to screen out a man in a rebounding situation. The teams that play intelligently are aware of all the circumstances at work on the floor—who has a sore ankle and can be driven on, who has four fouls, who cheats on defense so he can sneak down the floor for an easy breakaway lay-up.

Playing intelligently also means knowing how to take advantage of tactical situations: when to give up a foul or when to keep the ball away from a poor foul shooter on your own team when it's late in the game and the other team is obviously going to foul intentionally.

Sharman: Even in professional basketball, on a level where many players think they've learned all there is to know, the intelligent player is the one who never stops working. A good example is Bill Bridges, who was so important to the Los Angeles Lakers during the 1973–74 season. At that time Bridges was thirty-five years old and was playing his thirteenth season of professional basketball. He wasn't a starter for us; he had naturally lost some of his quickness and other physical assets.

But I'll never forget how Bill Bridges would sit on the bench and study the game situations, analyzing the opponent he was about to face and what he felt would work against him. When I called upon Bridges he delivered almost every time. And I definitely feel it was because he relied on his intelligence. He didn't just let his physical abilities dwindle and spend his time as a reserve who rarely sees action. When he got into the game, he was ready to play, and there were many times that I used him at center, even against a man like Kareem Abdul-Jabbar, who is at least six inches taller. I also used Bridges at guard in other games, even though his normal position was forward. Bill Bridges is a perfect example of a man who got smarter as he played, and it was definitely this intelligence that prolonged his great career.

Wooden & Sharman:

Learning to play intelligently is especially important to someone who lacks natural physical skills like quickness, a shooting eye or height. There's still room in basketball for a smaller player, if he's willing to work hard and dedicate himself to understanding subtle situations about the game that will give him extra insight.

Wooden: Mike Warren was only 5 feet 10 when he played for me back in the Lew Alcindor era at UCLA, 1965–68. Mike is the type of player who can serve as a model of encouragement to some of the young men who think that they might not make it in basketball. I consider Mike Warren one of the smartest players I've ever had in my entire coaching career. He is a player who made very few mistakes. His teammates loved to play with Mike

Mike Warren one of the most intelligent players ever coached by John Wooden at UCLA. He was always alert, rarely made a wrong move and other players responded to him. If they got open, Mike Warren would get the ball to them.

because they knew if they got open, Mike would get them the ball. He could get the ball to someone on either the right or left side. Generally, players pass only when they see someone open, or maybe they're only good at passing and seeing primarily one side of the court.

But Mike could do it all, and if someone was open on the court, anywhere at all, Mike would deliver the ball to him.

Mike would not be one who would look for his shot, but his selection of shots was excellent. He always had a good shooting percentage. He never took shots that were out of his range. He knew his area and didn't try to force them. He never took a shot if someone else was in a better shooting position.

You see, it's not that a lot of players who force shots are selfish. It's that they have "tunnel vision." This can give a player a bad reputation. Even though they're not trying to be greedy, their teammates will naturally feel hurt if they don't get the ball when they're in a better position and have a better shot. Actually, my players don't have to worry about this very much; they find out very quickly that players who approach the game selfishly don't play very much for me.

Sharman: When I first came into professional basketball I played against Al McGuire. He was with the New York Knicks and I remember him very well because I was impressed with his intelligence. That's how he was able to get into pro basketball, and I'm sure that's how he managed to have an outstanding career at St. John's. Al McGuire didn't have a lot of natural basketball ability. He wasn't a good shooter, he had just average quickness and there was hardly anything that set him apart from hundreds of other players. But Al McGuire made it to the highest level of basketball because he was extremely intelligent, one of the smartest players I've ever seen. He studied the game, studied the men he would by playing against and was always seeking that advantage, always trying to figure out a way he could make himself a better basketball player.

Without this intelligence he would never have been able to succeed. And right now, Al McGuire is one of the nation's finest coaches. He's been at Marquette for several years, and wherever he's coached, his teams are contenders for championships. I know that Al McGuire turns out not only good basketball players but smart ones as well.

Wooden & Sharman:

You don't have to play to learn the game of basketball. You can learn by watching. If you start out slowly and have to put in some bench time, watch the game and imagine what you'd do if you were in the game in that situation. Remember, too, it's not always the great athletes who succeed. People who observe and prepare can cancel out superior athletic ability with knowledge, preparation and cleverness.

Sharman: Watch other players and scout them well. Is your opponent left-handed? Does he drive to his left too often? If so, you can overplay him to your right. Is he a poor driver? If so, you can overplay him. Is he a weak foul shooter? If so, you can play him more aggressively than you can a man who's a high-percentage free-throw shooter.

Temperament is an underrated aspect of the game. Watch your opponent to see if he's got quite a temper, if he's hotheaded. Can he be rattled easily? Even if you're not playing, perhaps you can rattle him from the bench and hinder his effectiveness on the floor. Likewise, it's important not to have "rabbit ears" yourself. There are too many ways to get beat on the floor without letting words interfere with your playing.

As basketball fans, it's natural to cheer a great drive, jump shot or pass, or some other outstanding individual efforts. But our admiration for a superlative individual play often distorts our perspective on what's really happening on the floor, and might cause us to miss the important reasons why one team is superior to another team over the course of a game.

Great plays are interesting to watch, but a game is composed of a continuing series of events, and the teams that perform efficiently over the course of a game will be more effective. It might be a cliché but you'll hear words to the same effect from every coach you have: behind every great play is an unseen play that made it possible.

You can make yourself an essential member of the team by learning to perform these unsung acts with dedication, enthusiasm and consistency. By learning the game and by using your head, you can set the picks, make the defensive switches, fire the quick but unspectacular passes that make your team play better throughout the game. Doing these things consistently will help your team more than firing off twenty-footers at will. Screening out your man may let a teammate get the rebound. Keeping your hands up on defense may prevent your man or someone else from making the pass he could have made. You don't have to steal balls to be a great defensive player, and you don't have to throw wrap-around-the-back passes to lead the offense.

Wooden: I keep track of all forms of assists, not only offensive assists leading to baskets, but also defensive assists. That means whenever you help a teammate on defense, you get credit for an assist. You don't have to go over and block a shot. You may shift over and control a man, slow him down until your teammate can recover and get to him. In other words, for a few seconds you may actually be guarding two men.

As far as offensive assists go, many people (including official statisticians) think that an offensive assist must come from a man passing the ball to another man who immediately scores. Well, I also count screens as offensive assists. I think you are assisting your teammate on that just as much as if you gave him a pass. I know these aren't assists that count in official rankings, but I think they're just as important as the assists that do count. Even passes that don't count officially go into my record book. For example, a man gets the ball off the backboard and clears it out to a man who in turn throws it to a teammate for a basket. I'll give them both an assist. Two men, in my opinion, deserve credit for the same basket.

In fact, I'll give a man an assist on a play that doesn't produce a basket. That's another thing that doesn't count in official records; officially, the basket must be scored for a man to be credited with an assist. But in my opinion, it's not the fault of the man who made the nice pass. Why shouldn't he get credit just because the ball happened to roll off the rim . . . or his teammate missed an easy lay-up? There are many kinds of assists—screening assists, passing assists, rebounding assists, defensive assists—and I want my players to get full credit for them.

Wooden & Sharman:

Needless to say, developing your mind doesn't automatically result in better basketball play. And just because you play basketball, that doesn't mean you're going to get smarter. It all blends together, of course, the sharpening of mental and physical abilities. But one thing remains constant: the most important element of your school years is the pursuit of an education. Basketball shouldn't be anyone's total life. The relatively few players in professional basketball are the only ones who manage to make a living out of basketball.

Many great college players have been drafted high by the pros, only to live very short lives with professional teams. And even the ones who play for years have to make a living once they get into their middle thirties and start to slow down. As Socrates lectured to his pupils, knowledge is the most noble pursuit.

Wooden: The players who have played under me at UCLA will attest that, beyond any doubt, I've always stressed academics. I place the student's academic life *first*. That's why he's at UCLA, to get an education. If he doesn't desire that above all else, he doesn't belong there in the first place.

I'm very proud of the fact that basketball lettermen at UCLA have one of the nation's highest graduation rates, considering students on athletic scholarship. It's not by accident, because I stress the importance of completing college.

Not only is education important for its own sake, but it helps basketball players by giving them better perspectives on life. I sometimes think that my players will be better if they manage to keep the game in its proper place. If they put it above all else, they'll tighten up and won't do nearly as well as they would if they had the game in proper balance, as it relates to their life, their family, their friends and their other pursuits and goals.

Along that line, I do not encourage my players to play during the summer periods. I think if they're in a position to play and want to, then they'll play. There isn't a young man who won't, and I don't try to make any hard and fast rules against playing basketball. But some of the greatest players I've ever coached never touched a basketball from the end of one season until the start of the next season.

Of course, what's right for one isn't necessarily right for another. But I don't want them to feel that basketball is the one and only thing in life. They hear me say over and over that winning is the only thing. But they know I'm talking about basketball. In life, there are many, many other forms of winning that have no relationship to a scoreboard.

7 Fundamentals

Wooden & Sharman:
Every basketball player will have certain individual traits that will be distinctly his own style. A certain way of shooting free throws, for example, or a particular way of shooting his jump shot. If a coach sees that this style is effective, he isn't likely to change it. But there are certain fundamentals that are essential to playing good basketball and blending individual skills in with team play.

Sharman: I have been fortunate in coaching several ex-UCLA players. Gail Goodrich and Keith Erickson come to mind immediately, and I noticed from the start how well-grounded they were in the fundamentals of basketball. It was probably the most vital ingredient to their success as professionals. They were so far ahead of other players making the enormous jump from college basketball to the professional game.

I came to appreciate how well Coach Wooden schools his players in fundamentals, and how much importance he places on this phase of the game. It is certainly not coincidence that UCLA has more players in the pro ranks than any other school. I have had to cut former college All-Americans from my teams, mainly because they didn't have the proper fundamentals and couldn't learn them.

I remember hearing Sidney Wicks speak at a summer basketball camp and relate how much he owed to Coach Wooden for making him learn to play basketball correctly. I can recall Kareem Abdul-Jabbar explaining his ability to dribble, a skill most big men lack. Kareem said he practiced dribbling every day at UCLA because Coach Wooden insisted every player master the fundamentals of the game. It didn't matter what position he played or how big or small he was. The fundamentals of the game are the steppingstones to becoming a successful player.

Wooden: I discovered early that the player who learned the fundamentals of basketball was going to have a much better chance of succeeding and rising through all levels of competition than the player who was content to do things his own way.

A player should be interested in learning *why* things are done a certain way. The reasons behind the teaching often go a long way to helping develop the skill.

In addition to admiring Bill Sharman as a competitor, I have always recognized him as highly skilled in all phases of basketball. He was intent on learning the fundamentals and acquiring every skill required to master the game. I was particularly interested in learning his ideas on the teaching of shooting. He is one of the best pure shooters I have ever seen in basketball. He is a student of shooting and has become one of the acknowledged experts in this field.

Wooden & Sharman:

There are certain fundamentals which every basketball player should master. These will be presented as simply and concisely as possible, with detailed illustrations and photographs to assist the learning process.

Balance and body control

Balance and body control are important to every fundamental skill in the game. If a player is a good shooter, a good jumper, dribbler, defensive specialist—it means he has mastered the art of balance and body control.

The following points are essential to proper balance and body control:

- Keep your feet apart to establish a proper base—approximately the width of your shoulders.

- Keep your head over the base established by your feet—leaning beyond the base causes loss of balance and control.

Keep body low for good, quick stop, head and eyes up

Protect ball with body and arms

Maintain good body balance

Pivot on ball of foot

Stop—Pivot—Pass and Go

STOP

PIVOT

- Keep your hands above your waist and close to your body—reaching out should be avoided. Fingers should be spread but not tense.

- Keep your weight equally distributed on the forward part of both feet—not up on the toes or back on the heels.

- Your chin should be up to maintain balance and the widest possible field of vision.

Footwork

Balance and body control are closely related to footwork, and footwork is part of every important defensive and offensive move in basketball.

These are the essential points to learn:

- A sudden stop when you are moving at full speed is made by landing on both feet at the same time with the feet planted wider than the shoulders, your tail low and your head up.

Keep head and eyes up

Use quick, snappy pass—avoid lob

Follow pass with quick moves and cuts

PASS

GO

- Pivoting is executed on the ball of the foot and must be mastered since it is basic to many fundamental moves, which include protecting the ball, gaining rebound position, passing, screening and releasing, faking and driving.

- Quick footwork is a vital part of good fakes, feints, stops, starts, changes of pace and direction. You must develop quick foot movement.

- Stop before being driven into a corner or so close to the sideline that movement of your feet will be limited.

Ball handling

Did you ever notice what all great offensive basketball teams have in common? They have excellent ball handlers. The keys to good ball handling include the following points:

Fundamentals

- A quick release is the mark of the exceptional passer and shooter. Quickness must be accompanied by accuracy for maximum effectiveness. A good concept to remember is: "Be quick, but do not hurry."

- Handle the ball close to your body. This helps you protect the ball and maintain good body control.

- Handle the ball with your fingertips. Feel or touch is vital to shooting, dribbling and passing. Your keenest sense of touch is in your fingertips, not the palms or heels of your hands. Your fingers should be spread and relaxed.

- Generally, your elbows should be close to the body when you are handling the ball.

- Good vision is essential to good ball handling. Keep your eyes on the target when passing. Keep your head up when dribbling.

Passing and receiving

Every player likes to make baskets; every team wants to be a high-scoring unit. Both goals are related to passing. Players on a good passing team will get high-percentage shots, and this is the primary objective of a good offensive team each time it gains possession of the ball.

How do you become a good passer? It's not easy. Practicing shooting takes only a ball and a hoop, while to effectively improve your passing game generally requires other players. Perhaps this is why a good passer is known as a "team player," and passing could appropriately be called the most unselfish skill in basketball.

Here are some of the essentials of good passing:

- Your pass should be released quickly. Passes are usually made *by* defensive players, not over or around them.

- A quick pass is executed by a strong wrist and finger release. The elbows are seldom fully extended.

- Don't put excessive spin on the ball—it's harder to receive and control.

- Direct your passes. The straight pass should be chest high. The bounce pass should be between the waist and knee. Other passes should be directed to specific spots or targets.

- Passes must be crisp, neither too hard nor too soft.

- Be a deceptive passer—don't telegraph your plans. Don't stare directly at the receiver (this takes practice in using your peripheral vision).

- Use head and shoulder fakes, but limit your fakes with the ball. Ball fakes should be executed with the wrists, keeping the elbows close to the body.

- Be "floor-wise" with good vision.

- Don't hesitate with your pass. Know where the open man is, or will be, and get the ball to him.

- Don't force a pass. Turnovers will destroy an offense.

- Pass the ball, don't hold it. Don't slow down your team's offense and give the defense time to adjust.

- Move quickly after your pass. This will prevent the defense from playing you too tight and will help you get open for a return pass. The give-and-go is still one of the most effective plays in basketball.

There are certain standard passes which are used in practically every basketball game. You should learn to execute these:

- Two-hand chest pass

- Two-hand bounce pass

- Overhead pass

- One-hand push or bounce pass

- Hook pass

- Baseball pass

Head up, not leaning —

Fake with eyes—don't telegraph pass

Elbows fully extended for long or hard pass

Good outward wrist snap

Ball released off fingertips

Knees bent for balance —

Two-Hand Bounce Pass

— Weight on balls of feet

Hook Pass

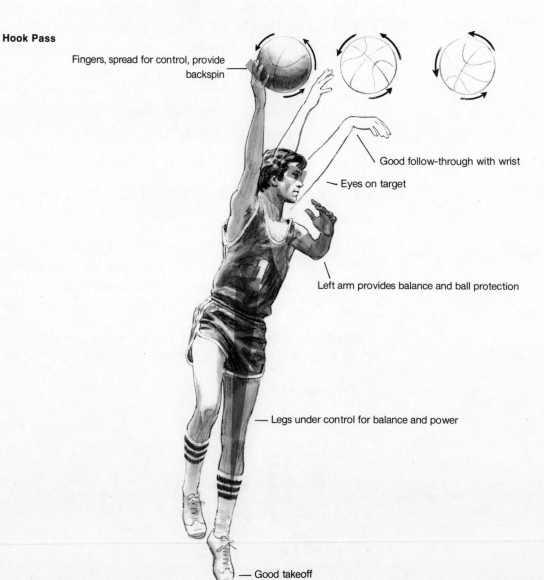

Fingers, spread for control, provide backspin —

Good follow-through with wrist

— Eyes on target

Left arm provides balance and ball protection

— Legs under control for balance and power

— Good takeoff

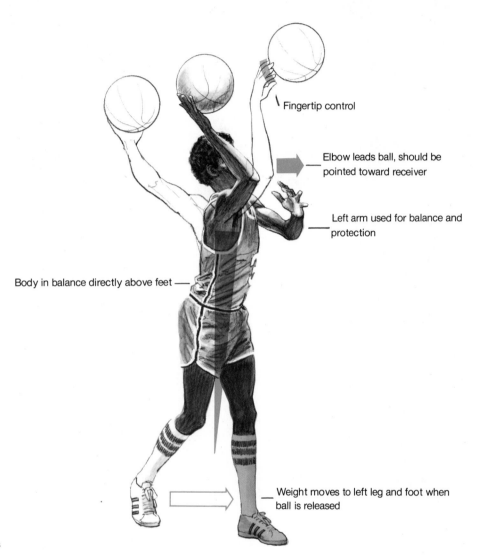

Fingertip control

Elbow leads ball, should be
pointed toward receiver

Left arm used for balance and
protection

Body in balance directly above feet

Weight moves to left leg and foot when
ball is released

Baseball Pass

Passer: Uses quick release after head fake up, passes close by defender

Receiver: Protects passing lane, provides target

**Quick Bounce Pass
Under Arm of Defender**

**Quick Pass Over
Shoulder of Defender**

Passer: Uses quick release after head fake down

Receiver: Takes wide stand for stability, protects passing lane, provides target

Passer: Uses quick crisp pass to target using open passing lane

Receiver: Provides target away from defender's pressure

Quick Two Hand Over Head Pass

Here are some essentials of receiving the ball:

- When receiving a pass you must watch the ball all the way into your hands.

- As the receiver you must get open at the right time for the pass. Provide the passer with a good target, a hand held up and away from the man defending against you.

- You must try to meet the ball with your hands relaxed. Don't fight the ball. Be prepared to protect it.

- You must get the ball before you can do anything with it.

Receiving the Pass

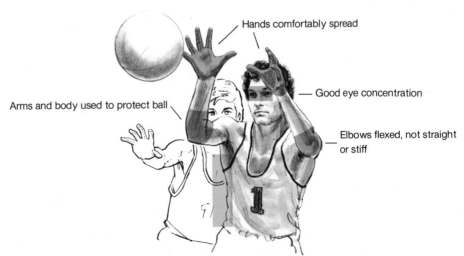

Hands comfortably spread

Good eye concentration

Arms and body used to protect ball

Elbows flexed, not straight or stiff

Ball on palms —

Elbow out too far —

— Knees too stiff

— Feet too close

Set Shot **WRONG**

Shooting

Putting the ball in the basket is the basic objective of the game. If you can't do this, regardless of all your other skills, you will not be a complete basketball player.

Anyone can shoot the ball, but the player who uses good judgment and does not force shots will become a higher-percentage shooter and will be of greater value to his team.

The Wooden-Sharman Method

How can you become an excellent shooter? Practice, practice and more practice. But make sure you're practicing the basic shooting skills correctly. Here are some fundamentals of shooting:

62

• Develop your own shot and practice it from the three to five spots on the floor where you will probably shoot in a game situation.

Eyes on target

Ball on fingertips and close to body

Elbow lined up with basket —

Head directly above midpoint of feet

Knees bent for balance and to help
generate power for shot

Weight on balls of feet —

Feet spread width of shoulders

Set Shot

RIGHT

- Once you have perfected your shot, work on a quick release as well as accuracy.

- Practice builds confidence, and you must have confidence in your own ability if you are to become a good shooter.

- In practice, as in games, don't force your shot. Stay in balance.

- You must concentrate to be a good shooter.

Fundamentals

63

After scoring you must give credit to the teammate who fed you the pass or set the screen which allowed you to take the shot. This may be done with a nod, a raised fist, a friendly tap on the rump or by saying "thanks" or "good pass."

A must!
Let your teammate know you appreciate his help
—a pass, a screen, a rebound, a switch—
by a raised hand, a smile, a wink, a nod...

Communications

Here are some basic shooting techniques which you should follow:

- Your fingers should be comfortably spread, the pressure being applied firmly to the ball with only the finger "pads."

- The ball must be kept close to your body for protection.

- The release must be made quickly, with the fingertips being last to touch the ball.

- The hand, forearm and elbow are lined up with the midline of the body. The elbow leads the shot, with the wrist cocked for the proper release.

- Your head should be centered on a line with a point between your feet. Your head should follow your hand up—but not forward—toward the basket.

- Shoot toward a specific target or spot, not merely in the general direction of the basket. The target can be the inside of the rim on the far side of the basket, or a spot on the rim closest to the shooter.

- The bend of the knees furnishes the force behind most shots. You must learn to use your legs in shooting.

- Usually, after releasing the ball, you must be in balance, ready for action, not falling away from or charging the basket.

Shooting—
Finger Placement

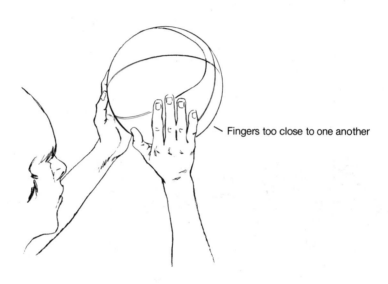

Fingers too close to one another

WRONG

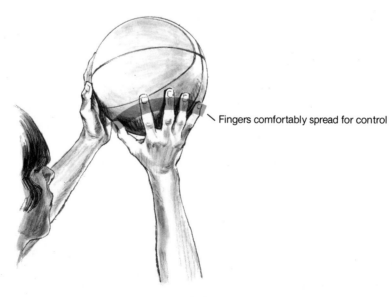

Fingers comfortably spread for control

RIGHT

Hand too high on ball

Ball on palm

WRONG

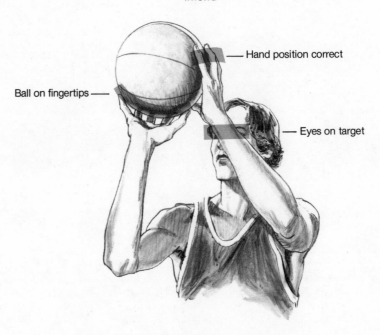

Hand position correct

Ball on fingertips

Eyes on target

RIGHT

Shooting—Hand Position

The jump shot has become the standard shot in basketball and there are certain considerations and fundamentals to be learned for this shot:

The Wooden-Sharman Method

- You start the set or jump shot from a balanced position, with the feet comfortably spread and the weight equally distributed. The weight is shifted slightly forward as the shot progresses.

66

- The body is aligned for the shot with your forward foot pointed toward the basket and your elbow close to the body.

- The shot is released above the head at the top of your jump. It should be the finish of a smooth movement, not as the final "jerk" of a two-part action.

- You should position the ball for this shot before making the jump. This eliminates extra movement of the ball during the shot.

- The best jump shot is made after causing the defensive player to be out of position or off balance. A fake often makes this shot possible.

Jump Shot

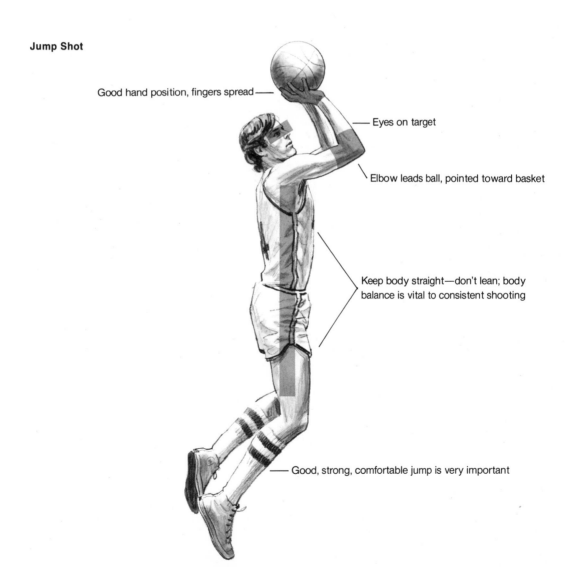

Good hand position, fingers spread ——

—— Eyes on target

Elbow leads ball, pointed toward basket

Keep body straight—don't lean; body balance is vital to consistent shooting

—— Good, strong, comfortable jump is very important

Jump straight up, maintaining good balance

Line up elbow with target —maintain concentration

Fake drive before shooting, keeping ball close to body

Bend knees while executing fake

Recover quickly to starting position

Fake—Recover—Jump and Shoot   (3) JUMP AND   (4) SHOOT   (2) RECOVER   (1) FAKE

The closer you are to the basket, the better your chances are of making the shot. The highest-percentage shot of all is the lay-up or the underbasket shot. Here are the special considerations concerning this shot:

- You want height from your jump, not distance, when you go up for a shot near the basket. However, avoid straining so much for height that you lose accuracy in making the shot.

- Protect the ball with your non-shooting arm, but don't pull your hand away so early that you lose control of the shot.

- Finish the shot with your palm toward the basket. Your hand can be under the ball or behind it.

- Take off on the foot opposite the shooting hand. For a left-handed shot, take off on the right foot, and vice versa. Concentrate on the target. The lay-up is generally made in heavy traffic and you must not be distracted.

Rebounding

The team that controls the backboards usually controls and wins the game. The player who is an excellent rebounder is an asset to any team, yet rebounding is a skill to which many players do not give much thought.

First let's deal with the general considerations involved in rebounding:

- To become a good rebounder you must assume that *every* shot will be missed. Be determined to get the ball.

- You must constantly work to gain position on your opponent for rebounding.

- Time your rebound and *explode* so that you reach the ball at the peak of your jump, with your arms fully extended.

- You should always prepare to rebound with your hands up (above your shoulders) and your elbows out.

Protect ball with body and inside arm and elbow

Take off on inside foot

The Lay-up

Release ball from hand opposite takeoff foot —

Keep eyes on target

High jump to basket—rather than broad jump

In establishing position, defensive
player knows where opponent and ball are
at all times

When shot is taken, defensive man turns
in front of opponent, raises hands above
shoulders with elbows out and tail low

Rebounding

Here are some special considerations for offensive rebounding:

- Make your move for position quickly. A fake will often help you avoid being blocked out.

- If the defensive man has position, you must not climb his back.

- Since you know your team's offense and the style of your shooters, play the rebound angles off the boards.

Here are special considerations for defensive rebounding:

- When your man shoots, turn across in front of him and take one or two quick steps backward, blocking him—then go for the ball.

- If a player other than the man you're defending shoots, check your man by turning in front of him and stopping his charge before going for the ball yourself.

*The
Wooden-Sharman
Method*

72

Explode for rebound—go for ball, don't let ball come to you

In maintaining control, land with solid footing, legs spread; protect ball with body, arms and legs, keeping head up and eyes straight ahead

- When a shot is taken, immediately raise your hands over your shoulders, with the palms toward the basket as you turn, and with your elbows out.

- Do not allow yourself to be crowded too far under the basket. The lower your tail, the tougher you will be to move.

- When you get the rebound, jerk it to your chest and come down looking for the outlet pass.

Dribbling

Every good team must have at least one strong dribbler. The dribbler becomes vital to the team when the defense applies the press or a tight man-to-man defense. Dribbling is a skill which requires as much practice and concentration as shooting or any other basic skill.

Prepare to dribble or pass as quickly as possible; extend elbows, keep ball close to body

Here are some general fundamentals:

- Don't look at the ball. Keep your eyes and head up. Dribbling allows you to move the ball and only by *seeing* can you move with purpose.

- You *must* be able to dribble with either hand. The one-handed dribbler is a handicapped basketball player.

- Protect the dribble with your body and your opposite arm and hand.

- Control the dribble with your fingers and wrists, using the arm and shoulder for force. You must use a strong, pounding dribble when in traffic to prevent the ball from being easily deflected by a defensive player.

- When dribbling in congestion, you should use a low balance with the ball close to your lowered body.

- When dribbling for speed, you should keep the ball out in front with a high bounce.

The Wooden-Sharman Method

74

Head up, not watching ball

Waist relaxed

Wrist and finger control

Knees bent

**High Dribble —
Used for Speed**

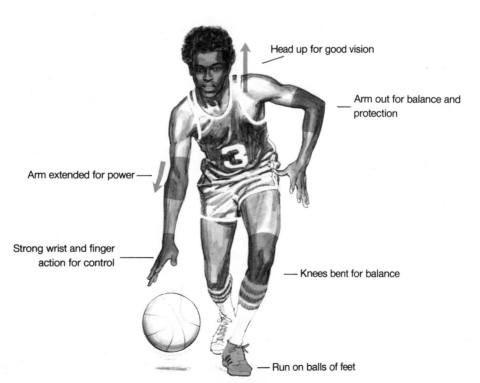

Head up for good vision

Arm out for balance and
protection

Arm extended for power

Strong wrist and finger
action for control

Knees bent for balance

**Low-Dribble —
Used for Ball Control,
Protection and Change
of Direction**

Run on balls of feet

Individual defense

Defense is as important as offense in basketball. Yet, many players become so concerned with the number of points they score that they neglect this vital aspect of their game.

Here are some points to remember:

- You must develop an aggressive defensive attitude. You should have the feeling: "My man won't score" . . . "I'll intercept the pass" . . . "I'll force him to make the wrong move."

- You must have personal pride in knowing that you play great defense.

- You must outthink the offense by anticipating their moves, by switching to break up their patterns, by not taking fakes.

- Know where your man is at all times. Know where the ball is at all times. Know where the basket is at all times.

Defensive Stance— When Offensive Man Is Beyond His Shooting Range

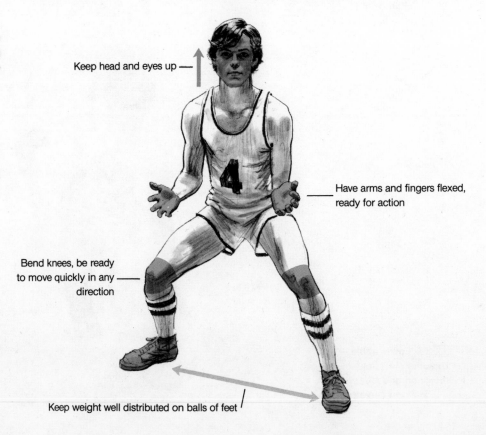

Keep head and eyes up —

Have arms and fingers flexed, ready for action

Bend knees, be ready to move quickly in any direction

Keep weight well distributed on balls of feet

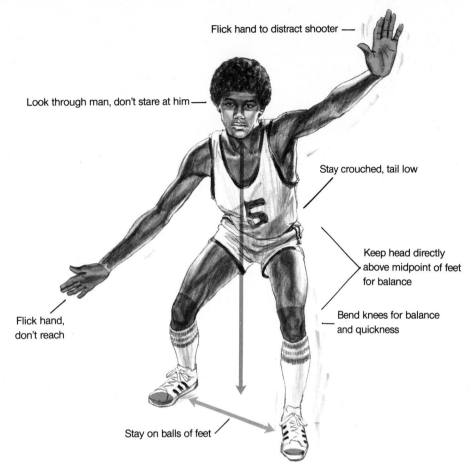

Flick hand to distract shooter —

Look through man, don't stare at him —

Stay crouched, tail low

Keep head directly above midpoint of feet for balance

Bend knees for balance and quickness

Flick hand, don't reach

Stay on balls of feet

Defensive Stance— When Offensive Man Has Option to Drive or Shoot

- Stay between your man and the basket you are defending. (There is an exception; when your man is under or near the basket, you may choose to "front" him to deny him the ball.)

- You should talk on defense. Yell at the shooter. Encourage your teammates, call out defensive strategies—"Watch the screen," "Switch," "I've got the shooter" and so on.

- Balance is essential to good defensive play. Do not bring one foot up to the other when you slide. Keep your feet comfortably spread.

There are some special considerations for playing defense when your man has the ball:

- Do not lean and reach for the ball. This is the easiest way to commit a foul, or to permit your man to drive by you, or pass and cut successfully.

Fundamentals
- Do not leave your feet unless the ball is in the air.

77
- Never give your man a straight drive to the basket. Force him to go around.

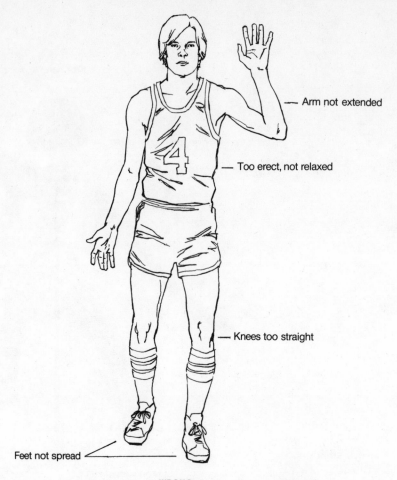

— Arm not extended

— Too erect, not relaxed

— Knees too straight

Feet not spread —

WRONG

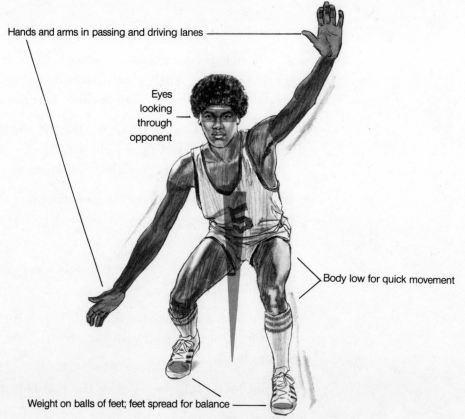

Hands and arms in passing and driving lanes —

Eyes
looking
through
opponent

Body low for quick movement

Weight on balls of feet; feet spread for balance —

**Defensive Stance—
Against Possible Drive**

RIGHT

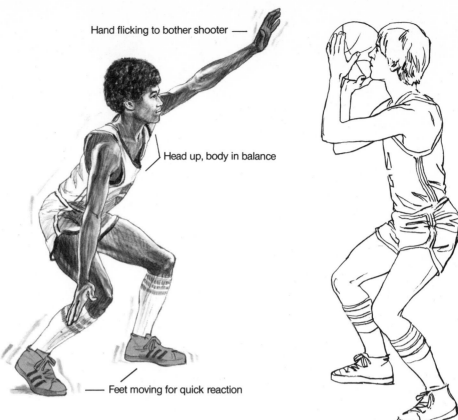

Hand flicking to bother shooter —

Head up, body in balance

— Feet moving for quick reaction

**Defensive Stance —
Against Possible Shot**

- When your man has the ball, stay an arm's length from him and avoid reaching for the ball.

- Never give your man the baseline for a drive.

- Keep one hand flicking in the passing or shooting lane and the other defending the drive.

- Use split vision. Make sure you see not only your man but as many of the other players as possible.

- Special considerations when your man does not have the ball:

- Make it difficult for your man to receive the ball when he is in a position to score or set up a score. The most effective defense is played before your man gets the ball.

- Play your man and the ball. The farther the ball is from your man, the farther you may be from him, opening up toward the ball with one hand pointing toward your man, the other toward the ball.

Fundamentals

To this point we have been dealing with individual skills, designed to help you become a better player. But basketball is a team game, as has been stressed throughout this book, and your success as

Play begins with fake, causing defensive player to move and look away from man setting pick

FAKE

Pick and Roll

a player will be directly related to how you mesh your talents with others on your team.

One of the most basic plays involving teamwork should be considered here. It's the pick-and-roll play. It's one of the prettiest maneuvers in basketball and one of the most gratifying to everyone involved. You'll understand completely when you and a teammate click on a pick-and-roll play that results in a basket. So will everyone else. Sometimes you'll even hear "nice move" from your opponents.

Pick is set in path of defender as drive
starts; picker must establish controlling
position and maintain solid balance

PICK

Dribbler drives for basket—if a defender
switches, then dribbler looks for a pass
to teammate

When picker feels contact, he rolls toward
basket immediately

Pick and Roll (cont.)   ROLL

Bounce pass is very effective in this play;
dribbler should not telegraph the pass

PASS

(*Left*) **Wooden:** Oscar Robertson shows excellent body balance against the pressure of a defender at the rear. Robertson's feet are well spread for support. The ball is protected and close to the body. The head is turned over the inside shoulder for good vision. **Sharman:** Not only is Robertson's form excellent, but from this position he can execute fakes before the shot or the pass. Sometimes he will fake two, three or four times before shooting.

(*Right*) **Sharman:** Jerry West demonstrates the correct way to pivot and turn a corner while dribbling. Notice how he protects the ball with his body, and has great body balance. **Wooden:** Very good form by West on the drive. His head is up, and his eyes are on the path ahead, not on the ball.

(*Left*) **Sharman:** Elmore Smith may be overdoing it here, but he shows the effectiveness of using the arms for body position and boxing out on the boards. **Wooden:** Abdul-Jabbar obviously feels Smith should be caught for holding. He's probably right because Elmore's arms are spread out in an unnatural manner.

(*Right*) **Wooden:** A good example of body control against pressure as shown by Jim Price. The ball is protected against the defender, the feet are spread well, the tail is down for a low center of gravity and the head and eyes are up. **Sharman:** Price also shows the proper position to make a dribble pivot. The elements are all correct—the footwork, body balance, ball control and ball protection.

(*Left*) **Wooden:** Abdul-Jabbar shows almost perfect form on this hook shot. The ball is well balanced in the shooting hand. The left hand is released and the left arm is protecting. The eyes are up and on the target. The body is in excellent balance and ready to spring.

(*Right*) **Sharman:** An excellent example of the proper form on a jump shot. Bill Bridges has his arm, elbow and wrist lined up with the basket. He has good body balance, and the ball is in good position for a proper release. **Wooden:** Bridges shows excellent upper body form. However, for better balance when he comes down, the feet should be spread a little to enable him to move quickly.

(*Left*) **Sharman:** A great picture of John Havlicek using body balance to twist around Bill Bridges, who has established defensive position. Havlicek makes sure he doesn't get called for the offensive foul. **Wooden:** Nice drive by Havlicek through heavy traffic. He uses the backhand layup wisely here, because coming in from the other side will probably result in a charging foul.

(*Right*) **Sharman:** Good body control by Darrall Imhoff as he uses a reverse layup to get around the attempted block by Wilt Chamberlain. Imhoff has the added advantage of being a lefthander, which comes to good use here.

(*Left*) **Sharman:** Gail Goodrich shows it's possible to shoot over and around a man who's at least 8 inches taller. Goodrich uses his own body for protection and releases the ball from his fingertips, with his arm fully extended. **Wooden:** Goodrich strains to get the shot off against Dave Cowens, but even in such a pressure situation Gail's form is excellent.
(*Right*) **Wooden:** This is excellent form for the hook shot as shown by Kareem Abdul-Jabbar. All the check points are "just right"—the eyes, the head, the left arm, the shooting hand and arm. **Sharman:** Perfect form for the hook. Sitting on the opposite bench against Kareem, I just wish Coach Wooden hadn't taught him so well!

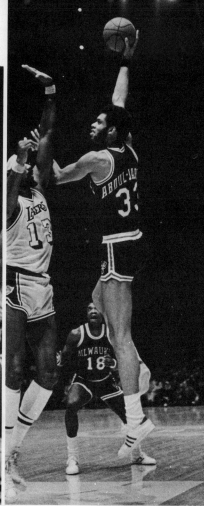

(*Left*) **Wooden:** Bill Bridges demonstrates good balance and body control. Notice the excellent hand and finger control of the ball as he makes the back-hand release. **Sharman:** Bridges shows good jumping position. You should high-jump to the basket rather than broad-jump. This allows you to get much higher and maintain better body balance.
(*Right*) **Wooden:** Abdul-Jabbar shows fine body balance in heavy traffic and excellent fingertip release. **Sharman:** He also shows good protection of the ball with his left arm. It's a shot almost impossible to stop.

(*Left*) **Sharman:** Aggressive and determined rebounding as shown by Happy Hairston of the Lakers. He keeps his eyes glued to the ball, a very important factor in rebounding. **Wooden:** Hairston has achieved excellent rebounding position. It enables him to out-rebound the much taller opponent.

(*Right*) **Sharman:** An illustration of why it's important to box-out your man before going to the boards for a rebound. Somebody forgot to take care of Bill Russell and he's coming over Darrall Imhoff's back to get the rebound.

(*Left*) **Sharman:** Gail Goodrich shows proper dribbling technique under pressure. His head is up for good vision, he has excellent body balance, and he is protecting the ball. **Wooden:** From this position you can be sure Goodrich will get a good jump shot, if he doesn't go all the way on the drive.

(*Right*) **Wooden:** An example of a pick-and-roll. Walt Bellamy has legally set a screen on Jerry West as Pete Maravich dribbles past. Bellamy is now in good position to roll for the basket and receive a pass from Maravich. **Sharman:** I feel Maravich's dribble is too high for maneuvering in traffic. A shorter dribble allows quicker moving and cutting, and affords better ball protection.

8 Practice Hints

Wooden & Sharman:
Making progress in basketball is identical to making progress in other walks of life; it takes hard work and patience. The best formula is to work at it a little each day, rather than pouring it on one day and not practicing at all the next day.

Basketball is a game that lends itself to individual work. We've stressed the importance of team play and how to act and react to others on the floor. But basketball skills are individualistic, and you can do a lot alone, or with a friend, to improve your talents.

Shooting

It's always good to set a goal for yourself when you're shooting. If you are working on free throws, your goals can be to make five straight before you quit. Gradually you should increase the goal—make ten straight before you quit, then fifteen straight and so on.

Do the same thing with shots from other spots on the floor. Make five straight jump shots before leaving . . . and then the next day, try to beat that record, make ten straight. Practice your shots from where you'll take them in a game. It doesn't do much good to heave the ball from half court. You aren't going to be taking that shot in a ball game. You probably have limited time to practice, so don't waste it.

Another good practice habit is to work on form before you start shooting. To do this, pick a spot on the backboard and hit that. Don't try to make the basket. Concentrate on fundamental form—make sure your elbow is in close to your body. Make sure you're releasing the ball quickly. Make sure the ball is coming off your fingertips and not the palm of your hand. If it is coming off the tips of your fingers, you'll get the proper backspin on the shot. You can check these fundamentals by working on form *before* you start your shooting drills.

If you're shooting with a friend, it's good practice to have him pass you the ball, then step back and put up his hand. He shouldn't try to block the shot, but merely have his hand up so you'll have to shoot over something. When your buddy raises his hand, fake, take one or two dribbles and shoot a jump shot. If you're practicing alone you can get the same effect by shooting over a ladder or some other object. You'll enhance your practice benefits by shooting over something. Bounce the ball off the wall or a garage door, and then have something to shoot over. It's definitely a different shot than when you're on the court by yourself.

Passing

When you're practicing alone, the best drill is to go into a gym and work on different types of passes against the wall. Don't work on just one type of pass. Work on everything—the two-hand chest pass, the one-hand pass, the bounce pass, the long baseball-type pass and so on. Work on accuracy. Pick a spot on the wall for a target and try to hit it with every type of pass.

Another drill is to use the corner of the gym, look at a spot on one wall and pass to the other. This develops peripheral vision. Again, make sure you concentrate on accuracy. Pick a spot and hit it. Work on being able to hit the spot without telegraphing your passes. Look one way and pass the other. Keep your head up while making these passes. Concentrate on keeping the entire court in your plane of vision.

Deception is a big part of good passing, and this must be practiced. You should learn different fakes and maneuvers, and you can work on these while passing the ball against a wall. Don't get caught in the stereotype of making the same fake before a certain type of pass. The defense will pick it up quickly. Work on various fakes and maneuvers and you'll find this is an excellent way of creating game-type situations while you're practicing alone.

When you have a friend to work with, have him defend against your passes. Make quick and deceptive passes against the wall, but make the ball go *by* the defender's body or *over* his shoulder or *by* his hips.

Individual defense

Conditioning is essential to playing good basketball. A player who wants to become outstanding must be in top shape. One of the best drills is wind sprints. This is a running exercise in which you build up to five or ten minutes of straight running, starting slowly and getting faster. You wind up the running part by going full speed for about thirty yards, then slacking off to about half speed for about thirty yards, then picking it up to full speed again. Do this seven or eight times and you'll discover it's the best method for building up speed and quickness, in addition to stamina and wind.

Good defense means quick stops and starts, quick jumps and being able to change direction quickly. A player has to be able to shuffle and move and react in all directions if he's going to be an outstanding defensive player. You can work on this by yourself, stopping and starting quickly, changing pace and direction on your own commands.

If you're practicing with a friend, have him do the dribbling and you can work on defense. Stay directly in front of the dribbler and concentrate on your footwork. Make sure you never cross your feet. Shuffle and move, but don't get your feet tangled up. Stay up on your toes and the balls of your feet rather than in a more comfortable, flat-footed stance. Being up on your toes will allow you to move quicker and react faster.

Another good drill is to put your arms down at your sides, or your hands behind your back, and play defense while your buddy dribbles against you. This will make you develop good body balance and footwork. By not using your arms you'll be working harder. Keep your body between your opponent and the basket. Don't cross your feet. Maintain good body balance at all times.

When you're working on defense with a friend, you can practice fakes and maneuvers as a defender. Put him on the defensive, even though he has the ball. Make the first move toward him. Don't let him get the ball down low in a driving position. Make him keep it up high. You can become the aggressor on defense, faking and distracting the dribbler.

Sharman: When I was playing with the Boston Celtics, K. C. Jones was my teammate for a number of years. I think K.C. was probably the best defensive guard who has ever played the game. I remember one night when K.C. was guarding a man who was having a tremendous night. Everything he threw up was going in, and K.C. just didn't seem to have any answer for it. The next time this player got the ball, K.C. put his hands down at his sides and started stamping his feet. The player was so startled he threw the ball away. Another time, I saw K.C. start waving his arms frantically at the man he was guarding, and yelling incoherently at him. He did anything he could to distract his opponent, to make him lose his concentration. K. C. Jones played aggressive defense, but his approach was not always what the opponent expected. That's what good defensive basketball means—take the initiative away from the offense.

Wooden & Sharman:

Dribbling

This is one basketball skill ideally suited for individual practice. First, get into the habit of practicing with both hands. Many players do what comes easiest—working with their right hand only, or in the case of natural left-handers, working only on that side. This is a big mistake. Later, when you get to college basketball or try to play in the professional ranks, you'll find it's a distinct handicap not being able to dribble with either hand and drive in both directions equally well.

Another good practice technique is to dribble with your eyes closed. It's hard to keep them shut, so it's easier to use a blindfold or mask. Practice moving in all directions, using both hands, and starting and stopping quickly. Train yourself not to look at the ball. Players who have to look at the ball while they're dribbling seldom see the open man. They don't have the vision necessary to be effective dribblers or passers.

When you're working by yourself in a gym, pick out different spots on the wall or read signs or be aware of other objects in the gym. This will encourage you to keep your head up and not look down at the basketball. It will also help to simulate game conditions, pretending that these signs or spots are your teammates, and you're looking downcourt trying to hit the open man. Peripheral vision comes through training, and it's vital to becoming a sound basketball player.

Another good practice hint is to make an obstacle course with chairs, wastebaskets, ladders and other objects. You can get in lots of work on dribbling around them, cutting in between them, practicing your cross-overs and other maneuvers. Don't forget to fake and switch hands with your dribble. The objects on the floor can act as your defensive foils. They'll help simulate game conditions, and you'll become a much better dribbler and ball handler than if you just worked on dribbling up and down the court in a straight line.

Rebounding

To be a good rebounder requires jumping ability, and this can be developed to some extent through exercise. Practicing exercises like the "jumping jack" or skipping rope will increase your skills. You can do imaginary rebounding for second and third efforts. Try to jump as high on the third rebound as you did on the first. Another drill is to reach with alternate hands — first the right, then the left, then the right again. This is an effective stretching drill and will increase your stamina.

When you're alone a good drill is to tip the ball against the backboard. You can start out by doing it ten times, then fifteen, then twenty-five and build up even higher when you can. Again, be sure to work on both hands and tip from each side of the basket. Use the right hand on the right side of the basket, the left hand on the left side. You can also vary this drill by catching the ball with both hands each time it comes off the backboard, instead of tipping it. Then throw it back and catch it with both hands, pull it down and pretend you're making an outlet pass to a teammate.

Another good practice drill is a jump shot from about ten to fifteen feet out. Try to make the ball hit the rim, so you won't know exactly which way it will rebound. Follow your shot and control the rebound. This is a habit you must develop to be a good basketball player. Assume that every shot is going to be missed. Simulate game conditions by going to the boards on every shot. You'll be surprised how much quickness and jumping ability you'll develop. And you'll also be surprised how many times you'll be able to beat an opponent who is stationary under the basket, even though he might be taller than you.

When you're practicing with a friend, a good rebound drill is to box him out—prevent him from getting the rebound after the shot. Have him take the shot from outside, and before you turn your head for the rebound, watch his first move. Make sure that you box him out—pivot in front of him and block him from getting the rebound. If you turn your head immediately to go for the rebound, and don't watch his move, a lot of times he will sneak beside you and get the inside position on the rebound. Learning to block out on the boards is one of the essential ingredients in becoming a good rebounder.

Wooden: The two players close to the basket, Bill Walton and Keith Wilkes, have good balance. Their hands are up, ready to rebound if the ball comes out of the basket.
Sharman: The players could probably have done a better job of screening out before going for the rebound.

Sharman: Good illustration of the jump shot showing wrist and fingertip control of the ball at release. **Wooden:** The entire body is in good balance. The shooter has excellent head position, releasing the ball perfectly off his fingertips.

Wooden: Nearly perfect form on the hook shot. Swen Nater has good balance, good protection with the off-arm, good fingertip release high above the head. **Sharman:** Perhaps the most significant point: His eyes are on the target, and he's concentrating on the basket. He's not concerned about watching the defensive man or watching the ball leave his hand.

Wooden: This is not the form I like to teach, because Keith Wilkes has the ball behind his head and body. But Keith could get the shot away extremely well from this position—and he could hit. I wasn't about to change him!

Sharman: Kareem Abdul-Jabbar shows his extraordinary jumping ability, soaring over everybody to block a shot. **Wooden:** The timing and body balance of Kareem makes this a remarkable picture. Everyone else seems nailed to the floor while he makes a great play.

Wooden: Walton shows outstanding rebound position: eyes riveted on the ball, arms well spread, body in balance.

Sharman: Another
outstanding example of
jumping and timing,
either for a rebound or
to block a shot.

(*Left*) **Wooden:** Bill Walton demonstrates one of his many talents: rebounding the defensive board and looking for the quick outlet pass to initiate the fast break. An unidentified player is blocking out No. 40 very nicely. No. 53 and No. 40 should have their hands at shoulder height.

(*Right*) **Wooden:** Bill Walton is in excellent position to receive a pass, and he's providing a good target for the passer.

Sharman: Walton's leg position is very good—well spread, feet firmly planted. No defender is going to move him off that post very easily.

Sharman: A great illustration showing how a defensive man should guard a player on the weak side. Bill Walton has his eyes on the ball, but a slight touch lets him know that his own man is within easy reach.

Wooden: Excellent defensive position away from the ball: good balance, good vision, one hand pointing toward the ball and one toward your man, ready to move quickly.

Wooden: Perfect form by Bill Walton in blocking shot cleanly. He maintains good balance, doesn't jump into the shooter and seems to be directing the ball to a teammate, rather than swatting it out of bounds.

Sharman: Determination! Despite pressure by two men, Walton gets two hands on the rebound — and he'll make sure he comes down with the ball.

Wooden: Henry Bibby shows good fingertip control of the ball, keeping it low for protection and making sure his head is up for good vision.
Sharman: Bibby is protecting the ball well — but the picture indicates he may be carrying the ball, a violation.

Wooden: A good example of moving to get position to rebound a close-in shot. Notice No. 54 blocking out his man, keeping his concentration on the ball.

Sharman: Excellent illustration of dribbling at full speed. His head and eyes are up for good vision; good body and arm protection of the ball; body in good balance.
Wooden: The dribbler has straightened up a bit as he gets in front of the defense. This will allow him to measure his step and take off for the layup.

Wooden: I recommend using the strong hand when under pressure. Greg Lee, a right-hander, preferred to shoot layups with his left hand. It's unorthodox but Lee perfected the technique and used his body effectively to protect the ball.

Wooden: Lee has completed his body turn to protect the ball and has extended well for a quick release. If he'd gone up with his right hand, the taller defender would have had a better chance to block the shot. Now, because he has to play through Lee's body to get at the ball, there's an excellent chance at a three-point play.

Wooden: In this picture Keith Wilkes is in good position to take a short jump shot, or fake one. Body balance is excellent.

Wooden: The fake has drawn the defensive man into an error—he's left his feet. Wilkes can now move in under him for an easy shot and perhaps draw a foul to turn it into a three-point play.

9 Three Ways to Win

Being a winner in basketball comes down, basically, to three things: conditioning, fundamentals and teamwork. *Conditioning* is something you work on every day. It goes beyond the basketball workouts; it includes eating and sleeping habits. *Fundamentals* can help make a person of average ability an outstanding basketball player, and the lack of fundamental soundness has prevented many a great athlete from mastering the game. *Teamwork* involves not only the working with other players, but the unselfish attitude that lets you sacrifice your personal goals for the good of others.

Conditioning

Practice habits are extremely important. The way you practice determines the way you will play. A player doesn't perform in a sloppy, halfhearted manner all week and then suddenly turn around with a completely different attitude for games. Intensity through hard work and desire will make efficiency second nature in game play. Make good use of your practice time—don't waste valuable moments.

When practicing, set goals for yourself. It helps you gauge your improvement. Free throws are the easiest element of the game to measure. Set it in your mind that you want to sink eight out of ten or eighteen of twenty free throws and work every day toward that goal. This is also important in shooting. Work from different angles and ranges, and work systematically. Keeping track of your progress will help you find your strengths and weaknesses.

A good aid in helping you keep track of your progress is to practice with friends. The beauty of basketball is that you can play by yourself, but it's still wise to work with others. That way you can use others as a barometer for your own progress. A friend can help determine what weakness you have—weaknesses you might possibly not see in yourself. Often you may think you're doing something right, but in actuality you may be developing bad habits.

Hard work is the important factor. Only you can really know if you're 100 percent in shape—not 80 or 90 percent conditioned. To attain the top level of condition it really takes to operate at maximum efficiency, it's important to work extra time. Conditioning is especially important if speed and running are the keys to your game.

Wooden: My 1964 UCLA team went undefeated and won the NCAA championship, even though we didn't have a starter over 6 feet 5 inches tall. One of the biggest factors in that record was conditioning, which that team had to the ultimate degree. Most of our games were won late in the first or second half, purely and simply because of superior conditioning. The players realized they didn't have the raw physical power to compete with other teams. We devised a pressing defense that worked exceptionally well, but it took hard work and the players knew they would have to be in better condition than they had ever been. They made this sacrifice and it paid off in a perfect season.

Top physical condition cannot be attained if the players aren't mentally conditioned and receptive to my ideas. Conditioning isn't just a sometime thing which can be achieved in a couple of hours on a gym floor each afternoon. It means around-the-clock adherence to good athletic habits.

Sharman: A coach can offer advice, but individuals must motivate themselves. You have to learn some things to do yourself to keep in condition.

First, you have to learn to take care of your body. That means good eating habits. You should know the basics of nutrition and vitamins, as well as the value of good food, so you can perform better at each game and in each practice session.

Second, you should acquire good sleeping habits. You should

know how much sleep you need the night before a game, how much of a nap or rest you need the afternoon of a game. You should know how to control your social activities so they don't interfere with your playing during the season.

And third, a player should know the value of "self-pride." I feel this is a big factor. It means getting ready mentally and emotionally for the game so you can do the very best you can in every aspect of the contest. Each person is different in this sense of preparedness. Some will have to be alone for several minutes before the tip-off. Some will need that pep talk from the coach at the last instant. Whatever it is you need for that mental lift, you'll know it and understand it for yourself, with a little time and experience.

Wooden & Sharman:

These extra-practice activities are just as important as in-practice details like quickness, body control and rhythm. All these factors go into the conditioning needed to perform at top level.

Conditioning is not only physical but mental as well. It means curbing your temper and your selfish tendencies and not letting anger get the best of you. By curbing these emotions, you develop poise and self-control, and that means you'll not only be able to perform better physically, but you can also prevent unnecessary "pressure mistakes."

You'll often observe college and even professional basketball players "losing their cool" in the pressure atmosphere of a big game, costing their team a technical foul. Conditioning your emotional state comes through developing your confidence and skills, so that unusual things that may arise don't interfere with your performance.

Wooden: As a coach, I try not to let my emotions take over when I'm criticizing individuals. I must make my decisions through reason, not emotions. Self-control is a delicate adjustment between the mind and body.

As a UCLA forward, Curtis Rowe was poised at all times. I define poise as just being yourself. Being yourself in any situation is not fighting yourself. Curtis is one of the most consistent players I've ever coached, and I believe the reason for that is that he never seemed to lose his poise.

Mike Warren also had this trait of emotional control to a remarkable degree.

Sharman: Never let a situation get the best of you. In every game, officials are going to make some good calls and some bad calls. Often a player will get into a situation where a questionable call can upset him so much that it throws off his entire equilibrium, affecting not only his own performance but also that of his teammates, who can't be sure of his actions on the court. So it is important that a player control his temper and develop a good philosophy about officials.

A player should learn to question some calls in a very friendly manner. A player shouldn't scream or curse at a referee. Officials are human, doing the best job they possibly can. And there's no way an official can call a game to the satisfaction of both sides. There are too many times when a play could go either way. It takes some understanding, but a player should realize this and even acknowledge a good call by an official. A little psychology can go a long way. Be careful how you say it. A sarcastic tone of voice will quickly defeat your purpose.

Wooden & Sharman:

Fundamentals

It takes much longer to cure a bad habit than it does to learn something right the first time. Many professional players still have bad habits they picked up in their formative years, and many wish they had worked harder on the fundamentals.

Young men who have outstanding ability may be able to be sloppy in learning the basic elements of the game, and still perform adequately. But they won't be using their full capabilities. Learning sound fundamentals can make an average athlete an important member of his team.

It's important to read basketball books, to pick up the basic things you should know to play the game. Analyzing yourself will help you to play at the peak of your efficiency.

Fundamentally sound players are disciplined players. They take only the high-percentage shots, make the sure, sensible passes and perform in the stress and strain of competition with all the mental and physical discipline they've worked hard to learn.

Wooden: Any young person who has aspirations to be an athlete should understand at an early age that the most valuable physical attribute he could possibly have is the quick execution of fundamentals. In shooting, for example, you learn that you must keep the ball close to the body, that you must get the quick release and that you must shoot quickly.

Just because a man is taller than you doesn't mean you can't outjump him. The smaller man has to make the taller man come down with a head fake, and as he comes down, you go up. That's the type of thing you can work on. There are other things you can learn to do to improve yourself, if you have the desire and are willing to work. You can learn rebounding by throwing the ball up on the backboard and jumping up and getting it. You can learn passing by throwing the ball against the wall. You can work on shooting so that you can release the ball quickly and with accuracy.

Patience is important. Good things take time, and that's the way it's supposed to be. Always try to do things properly.

While specific fundamentals are covered in other sections of this book, it's important to know that all fundamentals stem from basic body control and balance. The crucial factor in improving your skill in basketball is having complete control over your body and developing quickness.

There are several aspects of body control. First is knowing your center of gravity. Are you standing too upright? Are you crouched too low? What's your head position? Are you leaning forward? Backward? The player who was perhaps the best at body balance was Elgin Baylor. He performed twisting, turning, mid-air movements that would make many "fundamentals coaches" shriek in horror. But Elgin developed his body balance past the point of conventional control. Most players won't attain that control and shouldn't try Elgin's type of body movement. But he had a common denominator with more conventional athletes—balance and body control.

Rick Barry is another player with very unorthodox and unpredictable moves, the kind that drive defensive players crazy. Despite all the improvising he does on the court, one common attribute is there —balance and body control.

Nate Archibald and Walt Frazier are two great dribblers. They drive, change direction, stop, rock, go, dribble behind their backs and through their legs; seemingly they do everything and anything. The closer you study and analyze these two players, you'll find one common characteristic—balance and body control.

Sharman: I remember when I was with Boston and we were playing for the World Championship in 1956 against St. Louis. In the closing seconds of a very close game, Bob Cousy went in for a lay-up against Bob Pettit, the great forward for the Hawks. He moved over to Cousy's right side to block the shot. Because Cousy had such great balance, he was able to shift the ball over to his left hand and still make the shot which turned out to be the winning basket of the game.

Earl Monroe is probably the fanciest, most unorthodox shooter in modern basketball. But he's able to go through some very difficult moves and get off "impossible" shots because of body balance. When analyzing a great shooter, you start from the bottom and work up through the whole body. Start with the stance, the feet, then to the legs, which provide the momentum and force behind the shot, and all the way through the arms and fingertips.

Sharman: Jerry West has the quickest jump shot in the game today. That's because he has the ability to plant his feet in a good stance so he can jump very quickly and be on balance. He wouldn't be able to do this without a good stance. A lot of players try shooting with their arms—pushing it instead of letting their body do most of the work. The longer a shot you're going to attempt, the more you should crouch.

You need the strength of your legs and your body to get force behind the shot. I'm sure everybody has seen a lot of smaller players like Calvin Murphy and Nate Archibald who can go out twenty-five to thirty feet and get the ball to the basket with great accuracy and control. It's because they have the knack of using their legs and body, rather than trying to push the ball with their arms.

Another important body fundamental to learn is the proper grip on the ball. Bill Russell complained that the reason he was never a great shooter was that he didn't have the proper coaching when he was growing up. He was never taught how to release the ball properly with the right grip. So he developed the habit of shooting with the palm of his hand rather than from the fingers. So as great as Bill Russell was, he never was a great shooter because he started out with a bad habit.

Still another check point is the elbow.

Sharman: It is very important that the elbow should be lined up pretty much with the basket. It should be in close to the body; it shouldn't be in too tight or too far away. But it should definitely be close to the body and lined up with the basket so you have a good follow-through. And when you follow through, make sure you're going directly toward the basket. You have to be careful in your follow-through not to let your arm cut across at an angle in a direction that is not directly pointed at the rim of the basket.

Jerry West and Oscar Robertson both have that elbow way up high in front of the ball, almost pointing at the rim, so they have the leverage when they extend that arm. When these fundamentals are present—proper leverage, the elbow up and a good stance—it almost insures another essential factor, proper backspin on the ball from releasing it off your fingertips.

If you don't have the right release, you come up with a stiff wrist and you will shoot a "knuckle ball" rather than a shot with good backspin that comes from using the wrist and the elbow.

I've watched many players who have tried to guard West and often they'll crowd Jerry to really stay right on top of him to stop his scoring. When Jerry goes up for that jump shot, he is fouled very often, and I know many players say one of the reasons he's so hard to guard is because when he goes up for the shot, he has that elbow pointing toward the basket. So when the defender goes up to try to block West's shot, he bumps Jerry's elbow and fouls him. Not only does keeping the elbow out front make for a better shot—it adds protection that helps get the shot off and makes it that much tougher for anyone to guard you.

Teamwork

Eagerness to sacrifice your personal interest or glory for the good of the team is one of the essential ingredients in becoming a successful basketball player. The team must come first. A team doesn't function solely on the performance of its stars; it needs the hard work of all its players.

For example, defensive players do not get the headlines that the offensive players, the scorers, get. But you have to have the outstanding defensive players if you want a good team. You have to have the good sixth and seventh man—and most of all, you need to have the depth that goes down to the last man on the squad. A team that practices against hard-working and fundamentally sound substitutes is going to be at its best most of the time. Unselfish team play is the key.

Wooden: I never want a player to score without thanking a teammate who helped him. Someone surely set the screen or made the pass that set up the basket. Or maybe someone kept an opponent busy and prevented him from floating toward the center to block a shot or help against the man with the ball. So I want a player who scores to acknowledge it—by a nod, a raised fist, a wink, a friendly tap on the rump—to the man who made the assist. It is natural for a teammate who doesn't get acknowledged to let up in his play subconsciously, or not to hustle as much to help out again.

The players must be interested in what is best for the team and be willing to sacrifice themselves. Keith Erickson was primarily a defensive player with my small teams of 1964 and 1965 and didn't receive as much publicity as Gail Goodrich and Walt Hazzard. But he was the key man in our pressing defense—the number-five man who plays the last line of defense under our basket. He did it knowing that he was going to play to make it possible for others to score. He truly exemplified team spirit.

Keith Erickson in action
for the Los Angeles Lakers.
John Wooden calls
Erickson one of the
greatest competitors he
ever coached at UCLA.
Bill Sharman coached
Erickson with the Lakers —
and agrees with Wooden's
judgment.

Team spirit often means having a prepared and exuberant bench. Not only must these players be ready to fill in and spell the starters, but they must sacrifice themselves to help the team in special ways.

Sharman: Pat Riley was not a starter for our championship team in 1972, but he showed great enthusiasm on the bench. He would encourage and fire up the team in the huddles, and, more important, he would motivate others by picking out small points about their play that even a coach couldn't see.

He shows great hustle on the floor and has the respect of his teammates because he has the strong enthusiasm so important to the game. It is extremely important to have this type of player who builds the team up with his enthusiasm.

Losing complex

Losing is just as much a part of the game as winning. Someone who wants to play basketball must prepare to accept both winning and losing. The truly successful person doesn't depend on winning to give him self-satisfaction, and thus he doesn't come apart when he loses. A winner in life is going to know how to lose.

A lot of athletes have been winners in sports but losers in life because they didn't know how to handle losing. To be a gracious winner, you must be a gracious loser—gaining this ideal comes from gaining dignity and pride in what you do well.

Wooden: Young people today are up against a lot of peer pressure. As coaches we try to realize it, but it's there and probably always will be. I think we're looking for a dream to some degree — we want to do well, and so many times we get judged by outsiders who rank us by our wins, our losses, how many points we score . . . and so on.

My method of trying to combat this is to convince my players that working hard and gaining pride in what they're doing is a way to gain satisfaction and peace. The more they let these outside factors influence them, the worse they'll do. It's better to work hard and enjoy what you're doing. When you get pleasure out of working hard and trying your best, you won't let yourself get down because someone outscores you. Instead, you'll study them and learn what mistakes you made and how you can do better. If you're really working at it and you can't do anything else, you're doing your best, and doing your best is success.

Wooden & Sharman:

Each day that you fail to do your best, you lose something that you can never get back. Make every effort to do the best you can — not because somebody else wants you to, not because you're expected to, not because somebody before you did. But do your best because of the personal satisfaction and pleasure you can get out of doing a thing well — to the very best of your ability.

Three Ways to Win

10 Pyramid of Success

Sharman: It's difficult for me to recall exactly when I first became aware of John Wooden's Pyramid of Success.

I probably saw it on a chart or a blackboard in a dressing room or perhaps in a book. I imagine my first inclination was to pass it by quickly as just another set of dry principles and words that didn't have much meaning for me.

If that feeling existed, however, it certainly didn't last very long. I remember reading the Pyramid of Success . . . and then wanting to read it over and over again.

I found it engrossing and meaningful, not only to my career in the sport of basketball, but to my entire life. I tried to grasp the meaning of the words and the structure, and I know that I studied Coach Wooden's Pyramid of Success as avidly as any player or coach in the country.

The Pyramid is much more than a collection of blocks and words. It constitutes a set of principles that can establish a standard of life for all of us. No one is going to achieve perfection in every detail, but these ideas provide worthwhile aims and pursuits. Baron de Coubertin, the founder of the modern Olympic Games, wrote, "Victory is a lofty goal for which to strive." I feel the same way about the Pyramid of Success. To achieve, to improve, to climb a little higher each day—that's what the pursuit of life is all about.

Those who know John Wooden understand that the Pyramid of Success is far more than words and blocks to him. John Wooden *lives* the Pyramid.

When we started this book together, I definitely wanted Coach Wooden to share his own thoughts on the Pyramid of Success . . . and I'm very glad he consented.

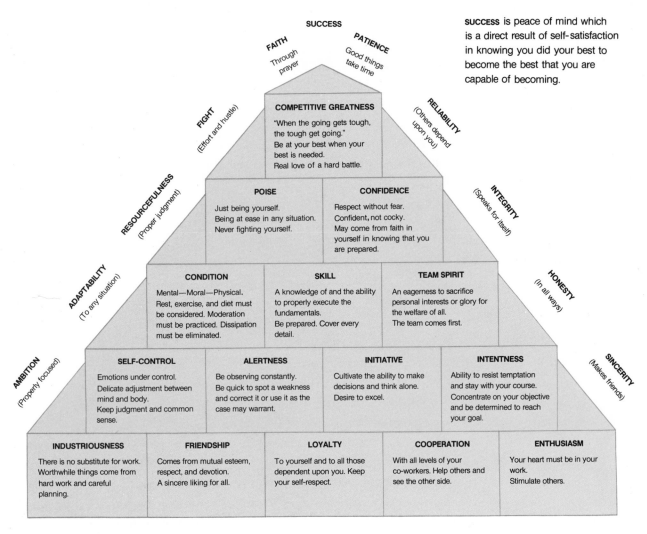

SUCCESS

FAITH
Through prayer

PATIENCE
Good things take time

SUCCESS is peace of mind which is a direct result of self-satisfaction in knowing you did your best to become the best that you are capable of becoming.

FIGHT
(Effort and hustle)

RELIABILITY
(Others depend upon you)

COMPETITIVE GREATNESS
"When the going gets tough, the tough get going."
Be at your best when your best is needed.
Real love of a hard battle.

RESOURCEFULNESS
(Proper judgment)

INTEGRITY
(Speaks for itself)

POISE
Just being yourself.
Being at ease in any situation.
Never fighting yourself.

CONFIDENCE
Respect without fear.
Confident, not cocky.
May come from faith in yourself in knowing that you are prepared.

ADAPTABILITY
(To any situation)

HONESTY
(In all ways)

CONDITION
Mental—Moral—Physical.
Rest, exercise, and diet must be considered. Moderation must be practiced. Dissipation must be eliminated.

SKILL
A knowledge of and the ability to properly execute the fundamentals.
Be prepared. Cover every detail.

TEAM SPIRIT
An eagerness to sacrifice personal interests or glory for the welfare of all.
The team comes first.

AMBITION
(Properly focused)

SINCERITY
(Makes friends)

SELF-CONTROL
Emotions under control.
Delicate adjustment between mind and body.
Keep judgment and common sense.

ALERTNESS
Be observing constantly.
Be quick to spot a weakness and correct it or use it as the case may warrant.

INITIATIVE
Cultivate the ability to make decisions and think alone.
Desire to excel.

INTENTNESS
Ability to resist temptation and stay with your course.
Concentrate on your objective and be determined to reach your goal.

INDUSTRIOUSNESS
There is no substitute for work.
Worthwhile things come from hard work and careful planning.

FRIENDSHIP
Comes from mutual esteem, respect, and devotion.
A sincere liking for all.

LOYALTY
To yourself and to all those dependent upon you. Keep your self-respect.

COOPERATION
With all levels of your co-workers. Help others and see the other side.

ENTHUSIASM
Your heart must be in your work.
Stimulate others.

**Coach John R. Wooden's
Pyramid of Success**

Wooden: I think it might be wise for me to explain the origin of the Pyramid itself. Many years ago, I was somewhat surprised to find that parents of the youngsters who were students in my English classes measured the success of their youngsters and the success of the teacher by the mark they received in class. I knew that fans and alumni tended to judge the success or failure of athletic teams by their won-and-lost record, but I wasn't aware until I became a teacher how much emphasis parents placed on the grade that their child received.

The good Lord, in His infinite wisdom, didn't see fit to create us all equal, either mentally or physically. We all come from different environments, and it's well known that each environment does not offer the same opportunity. However, I feel we all are equal as far as having the opportunity to make the most of conditions as they exist for each of us. And if we complain too much about our situation and are envious of the other fellow, then we will not make the most of our own particular opportunities.

Therefore, I began searching for something to help me consolidate my own thinking and my philosophy as to what I should try to do as a teacher, whether it be in the classroom or on the athletic field. I began searching for some definition of success. I had a high school teacher many years ago who felt that success was something more than Mr. Webster might indicate it is. The dictionary tells us that success is based on the attainment of a position of power or prestige or the accumulation of material possessions. I also felt that this definition was not fair or adequate because of differences in opportunity and individual ability. After considering the subject for some time, I decided to use the following as my definition of success: *peace of mind,* which is a direct result of self-satisfaction in knowing that you *did* the best to *become* the best that you are capable of becoming.

This definition of success became the apex of a symbol I created to help express certain ideas which I felt should be shared with my students. The symbol was in the shape of a pyramid, and I called it the Pyramid of Success.

Industriousness

If any structure is to have true strength and solidity, it must have strong cornerstones. And one of the cornerstones that I have chosen for this Pyramid of Success is industriousness. There is no substitute for work. All worthwhile things come from hard work. They don't just happen. If a person is looking for the easy path, there is no way, in my opinion, that he will have a chance to make the most of the ability he has. There is no short cut to success.

I'm reminded of a player I had at UCLA a number of years ago, Eddie Sheldrake. Eddie was small of stature but big of heart, and he was a tremendous worker. I don't believe that I have ever known a harder worker than Eddie Sheldrake. It is no surprise to me that he is now a very successful businessman. He always did a lot more than the average person, never content to take short cuts in basketball or any other facet of life.

There is just no measuring the endless amount of energy that this young man put forth in everything that he tried. He became an All-American basketball player, most of it through sheer hard work. Because of his size (5 feet 10 inches) he couldn't take the easy path in anything he did. He would have had no chance or opportunity to develop into the tremendous player he became. And those patterns became indelibly inscribed into his life, as he achieved what I describe as success — peace of mind and satisfaction that he gave his best in everything he did.

Enthusiasm

The other cornerstone that I chose for the Pyramid of Success is enthusiasm. Your heart must be in your work. I believe as a coach it is necessary for me to truly love and enjoy teaching the game of basketball. If I am to stimulate other people, I believe that I must enjoy what I am doing. I believe stimulation of others does come from enthusiasm about what you're doing. I don't believe it's possible for you to work your hardest unless you have enthusiasm.

Freddie Goss, who played for me at UCLA, had this enthusiasm for the game of basketball. He is now a very successful college coach, and a great portion of his success is due to the fact that he can impart this spirit and enthusiasm to others. It's so much a part of his life that it becomes contagious to others . . . and that's why I feel enthusiasm belongs at the cornerstone of the Pyramid of Success.

Condition — skill — team spirit

I have placed three things in the heart of this Pyramid and I believe they are of equal importance to the cornerstones. These are condition, skill and team spirit. I think my 1964 UCLA team, which went through the entire season without a loss, despite having no starting player over 6 feet 5 inches tall, certainly had condition to the ultimate degree.

The players on this squad realized that they did not have the raw physical power to compete with many teams. They knew that they would have to do other things to compensate. I'll never forget this particular team and what they went on to accomplish. They were the smallest team, comparatively speaking, ever to win the NCAA championship, and it's safe to say there was no one who felt that this team had a chance of going all the way and achieving what it did.

I have been referring to physical condition, but I found out long ago that physical condition cannot be attained unless your players are mentally conditioned and receptive to your ideas. They have to discipline themselves. They must be morally conditioned if they're going to be able to attain and maintain top physical condition, because players can tear down between practices more than is possible to build up during practice. I know of many teams that have been able to overcome superior ability because they are in better condition. There is no doubt that as you lose condition, your ability to quickly and properly execute the fundamentals leaves you. Therefore, it is important that the individual be in good condition if he is going to contribute to the team.

The coach must organize his practices to produce fine physical condition along with teaching the individual fundamentals and team concepts, but the players themselves must conduct themselves properly between practices if they are to attain and maintain top physical condition. There is dual responsibility involved and you cannot get positive results without each side doing his part.

In the very heart of the structure I have placed *skill*. This means a knowledge of the fundamentals of the game and the ability to properly and quickly execute these fundamentals. This holds true in any profession, whether it's playing basketball or practicing law or medicine or anything else. In a word, you must know your stuff. You have to be prepared. You must cover every detail, thoroughly and completely, and in this way you will be utilizing your skills to the maximum of your ability.

The third thing I have listed in the heart of the Pyramid is *team spirit,* which I choose to define as an eagerness to sacrifice personal interest or glory for the welfare of the team. It can also be regarded as consideration for others. The team must come first. I have had many players who I think were excellent examples of this. One is Keith Erickson, who has had an outstanding professional career in the NBA.

Keith didn't get as much publicity as some of the others I had at UCLA, but he did what he could do best for the team at all times. He was a fine defensive player for us, but the defensive players never seem to get the headlines that the offensive players do. Still, you must have defensive players if you are going to have an outstanding team. And Keith was one of the greatest contributing players that I had on my first two national championship teams in 1964 and 1965. He was the key man in our pressing defense: the number-five man, the last line of defense. I think that is the most difficult position to play and the most important position of all. Keith did it despite knowing he wasn't going to have the opportunity to be on the receiving end of the scoring, which all players like so much. He merely made it possible for other people to score. He truly exemplified team spirit.

The other forward on that 1964 team was Jack Hirsch, a very valuable ingredient in the success of the team, and again an example of an unselfish player. Jack was a player who contributed what he could do best for the team and realized that the scoring, for the most part, was going to be wrapped up by our two guards, Walt Hazzard and Gail Goodrich. They both went on to fine careers in professional basketball, so it's obvious they were outstanding players and scorers. But they would not have had the opportunity to become All-Americans at UCLA if our forwards and center hadn't contributed in their own way.

If anything happens to disrupt the philosophy that we are trying to develop as a team, then no one scores quite as much and the team suffers. In other years, when I had forwards such as Curtis Rowe and Sidney Wicks, our style changed a bit and then our guards had to understand that. There are times when my center has been the big scorer. The players must be interested in what is best for the team and they must be willing to sacrifice themselves for the team.

Steve Patterson, on my championship team for two years, 1970 and 1971, did that extremely well. And yet when we came to the championship game in 1971 against Villanova, when their defense was stacked to stop Wicks and Rowe, these two players again showed the team spirit that I like to see by feeding Patterson, and he scored more than he had ever scored for us before.

Lew Alcindor, or Kareem Abdul-Jabbar as he prefers to be called now, and Bill Walton were very unselfish players who helped the team as a whole. And even though we built the teams around their particular and special abilities, the teams would not have been successful unless they themselves had been unselfish and cooperative.

We must have *unselfish team play.* I want our players to look for the pass first and the shot second. I believe that builds up team spirit. I try to get the idea of team spirit across in many ways. I have many little sayings such as "You cannot live a perfect day without doing something for someone else without thought of repayment." It has also been written that there's a mystical law of nature that the three things that mankind craves most—freedom, happiness and peace of mind—cannot be attained without giving them to someone else.

I point out to my players that all rewards come from giving. Any honor that you receive will come from what you give. You must give to receive. It holds true in basketball and it holds true in life.

*The
Wooden-Sharman
Method*

120

Self-control

Another block in the Pyramid that is extremely important is self-control. Self-control means that you must keep your emotions under control. Neither player nor coach must permit his emotions to make decisions for him. As a coach, I must not permit my emotions to take over when I'm criticizing individuals. I must make my decisions based on reason, not emotion. I must be very careful and not act out of fear. Fear is an emotion and it cannot be reasonable.

Self-control is a delicate adjustment between the mind and body as far as the physical actions that we perform. If a player doesn't have self-control, then he will not shoot well, he won't play defense as well as he can, and he will make little, careless mistakes. You have to keep your judgment and act with good common sense if you expect to be able to function to the best of your ability and execute well.

I have had many players who had great ability but it took them a little while to get this ability under control. I think Sidney Wicks, at the time he came to UCLA, had about as much physical ability as anyone that I have ever had at a similar stage. But at the time he came to UCLA he did not have this under control and he could not put it to use for the best interest of the team. This was a little difficult for Sidney to understand at first. But as he came to understand it, and got self-control, he became one of the best, if not the very best, players in the country at his particular time. Be it understood that Sidney was not a selfish player, but merely undisciplined.

I've had many other players who, for a while, had a problem of getting their emotions under control, and they themselves know how much they improved once they were able to accomplish this particular thing.

Alertness

Alertness is another thing that I have chosen to place in the Pyramid of Success. You have to constantly be alert and be observing. You have to be quick to spot a weakness and quick to correct it or use it to advantage, as the case may warrant. As I mentioned earlier, Mike Warren was a player who many people thought was too small for collegiate basketball. He wasn't even recruited by many college coaches when he graduated from high school, because he was only 5 feet 10 inches tall and weighed just 155 pounds.

But Mike Warren was one of the most alert players that I have ever coached and, of course, he had the intelligence to go along with it. Alert people are usually intelligent and able to take advantage of weaknesses and capitalize on opportunities. They make opportunities through their alertness. Mike Warren certainly had this ability.

Mike Warren stands out in my mind as one of the smartest, most alert players I have ever coached, or seen, in college basketball. The young man many felt was too small to play the game became one of the most important members of two straight national championship teams.

Initiative

Another block I have chosen is initiative. You must cultivate the ability to make decisions and to think alone. The desire to excel has to be there for you to attain the goal.

Gail Goodrich comes to mind as an example. He was an intense competitor, and he had initiative. I'll never forget our championship game against Michigan in 1965. Keith Erickson was playing despite a pulled muscle in his leg, but Keith wasn't able to function to the best of his ability. He was a vital member of the team, the best defensive player, the key to our pressing defense.

Goodrich took over. He had the initiative to do the job and, of course, he had the confidence to go along with it. If you do not have this confidence, you will be afraid to act on your own. Goodrich exemplified this in many other ways, as he has demonstrated by his play in professional basketball. Despite his lack of size he has become one of the best guards of all time. It truly pleased me to see him selected along with Walt Frazier as an All-Pro guard in 1974.

Intentness

Another block in the Pyramid that I consider to be most important is intentness. I'll never forget my first year at UCLA. We came down to the final two games of the season needing to win them both to clinch the conference championship outright. Had we split these two games we would have been tied with our archrival, USC. We went into these two vital ball games with three of our starters out. Allen Sawyer had an emergency appendectomy. The captain and starting guard, Ron Pearson, was out with the flu, as was a starting forward, Chuck Clustka.

When you go into the last two games of your season against your top rival, needing to win both games, you know you're in a rather tense position. At that time a coach needs his best and most experienced players available. I had three youngsters who hadn't played much, although they had helped us a great deal during the year by coming in and serving as relief men for these three starters. Eddie Sheldrake replaced Pearson at guard and Paul Saunders replaced Clustka, while Ralph Joeckel played in Sawyer's spot. These three players, thrown into the breach at such an important time, played with as much intentness as I'd ever seen or could expect. And I think that, and that alone, enabled us to win both of those games from the USC Trojans.

They were very difficult games, because we were playing a fine team. But I've never seen more intent players than we had. It wasn't that they felt we had overpowering ability, but rather that they were determined to work together. We'd come a long way and they were just not going to permit themselves to be defeated in these two final games.

When I think of intentness I am also reminded of a guard who played for me in more recent years, John Vallely. John had played center in high school and had played forward in junior college. When he came to UCLA, I changed him to guard. There were many people who felt that he couldn't do it.

But John felt that he could and he had this grim intentness to prove to others that he could make the transition from center and forward to guard. He became one of our all-time fine guards. By the middle of his first year with us, his teammates started calling him "money man." This is a very high accolade for a player to receive from his teammates. It means, of course, he is at his best when he is needed most and is able to perform at his highest level in tense situations. I believe that he was able to do this through his intentness. John Vallely wanted to play so much he kept right on his course, working with as much determination as I've ever seen in a player.

I am also reminded of my championship team of 1968. We had lost a game that year, the memorable contest in the Houston Astrodome. The University of Houston, led by Elvin Hayes, beat our team, led by Lew Alcindor. The score was 72 to 70, and it broke our consecutive-game winning streak, which had reached 47 at the time. It was a tremendous game, seen by 55,000 people in person and several million on television.

We lost, and some of our players felt that our opponents, one player in particular, hadn't been too kind in his remarks after the game. I knew that everyone on our UCLA team dreamed about another chance to meet Houston. And when it appeared we were going to have the opportunity to meet them in the NCAA tournament, I don't believe I have ever had a team that prepared itself any better than this team did.

The rematch, in the NCAA tournament, was no contest. At one time in the second half, before I broke up the lineup, we led by something like 44 points. This was against a team that had not been beaten that year, a truly outstanding basketball team. The result of that game shows what can happen when you are extremely intent. I don't mean to infer that someone with no ability can have this intentness and determination and can perform miracles. That cannot be done. This UCLA team that I refer to had great ability *and* intentness. It's seldom that any individual, or any team, or group of individuals working together, can reach the maximum level of performance. But I feel this team did, and it was because of intentness and dedication to purpose.

That team played almost the perfect game. I believe it was their intentness that made it possible.

Confidence

Here is another block which I believe to be extremely important—confidence. I feel confidence is having faith in yourself, in knowing that you are prepared. You might have false confidence, a self-assurance you try to pass off as confidence. But I don't want *false* confidence. I want confidence that comes from facing yourself. I want my team always to respect our opponents, but I never want them to fear them. I want my players to have confidence in themselves, but I don't want them to be cocky or overconfident. Still, I would rather have my players a little overconfident than lacking in confidence.

I have had many players who had confidence from the start, a rather built-in trait. I have had many other players who had to work to acquire confidence. They worked hard on the other steppingstones or the blocks in the Pyramid, and ultimately they acquired confidence. A few years ago, when we were playing a team that had an outstanding scorer, one of my players asked me, "Coach, who's going to guard this guy?" I knew right then that he would not be the one, because of the way he put the question to me. It was as if he was asking, "Who's going to *have* to be the one?" I knew then he did not have confidence and I felt certain he could not do an adequate job against this man.

On the other hand, another player came to me and he said, "Let me guard him," and I said to him, "I think you'll get the opportunity because you seem to want it." That's what it takes. He did a fine job against this outstanding player, and we won an important game.

I like the player who rises to the task and has confidence that he can do the job. I want my players to have confidence, and I want it to come from a solid foundation of being in condition, knowing the job at hand, being mentally and physically prepared and imbued with the proper team spirit.

If a player has faith in the future and the patience to master the aforementioned traits to the best of his ability and is friendly, cooperative, loyal, resourceful and reliable, he is almost certain to be a poised competitor who will come close to realizing his full potential.

When that occurs, everything seems to mesh, and right at the top of the apex is the ultimate result — success.

Perhaps George Moriarty said it best in his poem "The Road Ahead of the Road Behind":

> Giving all, it seems to me,
> Is not so far from victory . . .*

If you do your best, it seems to me, no one can expect more. And, when you know that you have done your best, then you should have peace of mind, and that's success.

* George Moriarty, "The Road Ahead of the Road Behind."
